Country Topics

some essays by

Auberon Waugh

Illustrated by

Ken Taylor

London
Michael Joseph
mcmlxxiv

First published in Great Britain by Michael Joseph Ltd
52 Bedford Square, London WC1B 3EF
1974

© 1971, 1972, 1974 by Auberon Waugh

ISBN 0 7181 1250 4

Set and printed in Great Britain by
Tonbridge Printers Ltd, Peach Hall Works, Tonbridge, Kent
in Baskerville eleven on thirteen point on paper supplied by
P. F. Bingham Ltd, and bound by Dorstel Press
Harlow

Preface

There is a tendency to describe the countryside in terms of badgers, voles, rare and beautiful plants. Of course these things are there if one looks for them, but they play only a limited part in the life of the country. To discuss the countryside in terms of its flora and fauna is to accept it at its urban valuation as a minor amenity, rather like the zoo but without the same recreational facilities.

The main problem of country life is not how to protect the badger but how to avoid boredom. Badgers may be required to assist in the matter : either as the quarry in furtively organised badger digs; or as the rallying point for Badger Protection Societies and Save the Badger Action Groups. The countryside can also offer various other forms of cruelty to animals and corresponding opposition to them by way of entertainment : Staghunting and demonstrating against it; shooting at wild birds and feeding them with coconut halves and breadcrumbs. But by far the greater part of boredom-avoidance involves fellow-human beings : scurrilous gossip, bingo, whist drives, complaints to the local authority, feuds with neighbours. Where there are any children left, they devote their time to harassing the old and retired; there is also the important national sport of major-baiting, directed against the innumerable retired majors who have settled like a flock of starlings on every country village.

Few of the excitements of politics or world affairs reach the countryside, but their reverberations are sometimes felt. Readers of these pages may be puzzled by references to events which they have long forgotten in the daily excitement of metropolitan life – a power strike which occurred in the winter of 1971, a train strike in the spring of 1972 – but which left an indelible mark on the political awareness of the countryside. Britain's entry into the Common Market also leaves a mark, and so, bizarrely, do the troubles in Ulster. These essays are concerned with areas of the country where little is comprehended of the great events outside, and even this little is frequently misunderstood.

Other historical events are of purely local interest. Princess Anne's mysterious visit to the Junior Leaders' Battalion at Norton Fitzwarren may be discussed in the villages around for the next fifty years, but it never really made the national headlines; the same is true of Edward Heath's disastrous visit to a local government conference in North Somerset, when cows gave birth to seven-headed calves and milk inexplicably turned sour for many months afterwards.

Other historical references include the arrival of Asian refugees from Uganda, Picasso's ninetieth birthday, Khrushchev's death. The point of mentioning them is to show how these mighty events appeared from the backwoods. It would be absurd to say that the picture which emerges is typical. Mercifully, despite various attempts to present country life on the mass media, there is still no norm.

My only point is that the country does not exist in isolation; however unwillingly, it is part of the huge panorama of modern life. The purpose of collecting these essays in book form is not to satisfy an urban appetite for badgers, voles and dabchicks, but to show urban society what it looks like from this distant rural perspective – and thus, perhaps, to illuminate a neglected corner of social history .

My thanks are due to Charles Wintour, the enlightened and perceptive Editor of the *Evening Standard,* who commissioned these essays in the first place, paid handsomely for them at the time, and now allows me a second bite at the apple; and to Ken Taylor, who did the drawings.

COMBE FLOREY

APRIL 1974.

For My Children

Sophia
Alexander
Daisy
and Nathaniel,

all honour and glory through
the ages.

The day the bale-loader turned nasty

Combe Florey, Somerset.
July is the month when country dwellers sit back and gloat.
We may miss the fun at other times of the year – the political
demonstrations, the Great Debates, the glimpses of lovely
Lady Hartwell by candlelight – but in July, everything
happens in the countryside.

Last week, my neighbour in Somerset had the most terrible accident. He is Mr Ian Fraser, director-general or
whatever of the City Takeover Panel, and a name to con-
jure with wherever men shout at each other across the
dinner table about money or sit looking gloomy and Byronic
about prospects for growth. Down here, however, he is best
known as a plucky and conscientious small farmer on the
holding he bought near Dulverton for his wife, a cousin of
mine.

This handsome and popular small farmer was driving his
tractor over the hilly acres in front of his farm when something happened – perhaps he suddenly thought of the
Pergamon Press, or Vehicle and General Insurance – and
he fell off his tractor. This much – he could always climb
on again – if he had not been towing a bale-loader machine,
which seized him, hoisted him twenty-five feet in the air and
loaded him with other bales of straw in a neat line.

Luckily, the accident was not more serious. After a few
weeks away from the Takeover Panel, Cousin Ian will be
back there panelling away with the best of them. As neighbouring farmers pointed out afterwards, if he had been
trailing a dung-spreader, he would have found himself
spread all over the beautiful Somerset countryside, and one
hesitates to think what a combine harvester would have made

9

of this brave and industrious man – which parts would have emerged as corn and which would be rejected as chaff.

But if ever again some smart City commentator tries to suggest that the officers of the City Takeover Panel are men of straw, my Cousin Ian at least will be able by his wounds to show that this is not the case.

Other accidents of the haymaking season are too gruesome to relate, but one man who had spent all day jumping up and down on a hayrick, woke up in the middle of the night and jumped out of the window. It begins to look as though we refugees from the Great Plague of London are rushing like lemmings to certain destruction among the baleloaders and dung-spreaders of the technological countryside, where even hay-seed now possesses many of the less agreeable properties of LSD.

Other frenzies from the capital reach West Somerset more slowly, but on the last day of hay-making I met a Somerset youth who explained disconsolately that he was in the Army on his way to Belfast where he would be shot at by furious Irishmen, with whom he had no quarrel at all. As a casualty of an earlier colonial war – Internal Security operation, police action or what you will – in Cyprus, I was able to reassure him that an awful lot of rubbish is written about the disagreeable consequences of being shot. It scarcely hurts at all, and you get a very nice pension afterwards. But this encounter did emphasise the absurdity of a situation where honest Somerset lads must be sent across the sea to be shot at because a few self-important politicians have got it into their heads that a part of Ireland is really a part of England. It might have been Timbuctoo as far as my friend was concerned.

The saddest part of this sad story is that his presence in Ulster, far from contributing to the peace, will obviously now only provide a focal point for more agitation. Any British government which was genuinely interested in keeping the peace would allow Irish troops to fulfil this task in the Irish areas of Derry, Newry, and Enniskillen while British troops kept the peace in the areas of Scottish settlement.

Meanwhile, the Irish have adopted what any Cyprus veteran could have told them is the only course of action which has never failed to get a British Army of occupation out. This is the disgraceful, shocking and utterly unjustifiable expedient of shooting British soldiers. Of course it is impossible to imagine any British Cabinet – let alone one which includes, for instance, Lord Hailsham – allowing Irish troops into Derry, at any rate until at least twenty British soldiers have been killed.

Talking to my friend in West Somerset, I just hoped that he would not be one of them. There is nothing we can do about politicians' attitudes on this sort of thing. But when you start hearing about it in the lanes and pubs of West Somerset, something must have gone seriously wrong.

Next week I shall probably describe the hideous scandal of the Wheatsheaf public house in Chilton Foliat, North Wiltshire. In order to save a couple of hundred pounds over the next thirty-five years, the brewery which owns it is trying to get permission to replace its beautiful thatched roof with tiles.

Thatched roofs are a feature of Chilton Foliat, one of the

glories of the Kennet valley, which is one of the glories of England. There is no prohibitive shortage as yet of thatchers or of thatching material, but if these wretched brewers are allowed to get away with it, so will every big landlord in the district. The brewers concerned have been refused permission for this outrage by the Rural District Council, backed by the Wiltshire County Council. Now they have appealed to Mr Walker's Department of the Environment, which sometimes seems to have a soft spot for brewers.

Unless I hear that the appeal has been dropped I shall name the guilty men and call for a national boycott of their bloodstained beer.

Flee — when the rich men come to roost

Chilton Foliat, Wiltshire.

The Village Hall, in Chilton Foliat was prepared as a court-room. The inquiry was held on a weekday morning, so few villagers could turn up. Perhaps the scene was little different from the Bloody Assizes of the great Judge Jeffreys during his tour of the West Country, but the judge on this occasion was an inspector from Mr Peter Walker's Department of the Environment.

While traffic thundered outside on the A419, a representative of John Courage Ltd, the brewers, stood up to explain why his firm should be allowed to replace thatch by clay tiles on the roof of the village pub, called the Wheatsheaf.

Chilton Foliat was not a particularly beautiful village, he said. It would be more accurate to describe it as a collection of houses along the road. Although many of the houses were scheduled and some were thatched, many more were not. He would call an expert witness to say that clay tiles were actually an improvement. Most of the village was owned by two big estates neither of which had any objection to the idea.

When he sat down, one received the impression that Mr Richard Courage, the chairman, was one of those misunderstood philanthropists, anxious only to combat superstition and relieve the primeval squalor of poor, ignorant Wiltshire villagers.

The position, I am afraid, seems different to the villagers themselves. They have been signing petitions and organising action groups for weeks. To them, it seems that Courage Limited is being both shortsighted and mean: despite record profits last year, it is prepared to wreck their village for the sake of a couple of hundred pounds.

Shopping for conscience is a tiresome business. I already motor for miles on an empty tank to avoid certain petrol stations, after the behaviour of some oil companies in the Nigerian Civil War. I try to avoid some Scandinavian goods out of a general suspicion of Scandinavia, and an obviously unjustified fear that they may be stuffed with contraceptives. Now I must remember whenever I am offered a glass of beer to ask if it is made by Courage, rejecting it with cries of disgust if it is. The countryside still means something to me.

But it is not to escape Courage's vandalism in Wiltshire that my wife and I, with four children, a dog, two budgerigars, a gold fish, a terrapin, etc., have decided to settle finally in West Somerset. The area is just becoming too rich. For some reason or other they have all settled in my corner of the Wiltshire – Berkshire border. There is Sir Charles Clore at Hungerford, Mr Hyams at Ramsbury, Mr Rothschild at Shalbourne, Mr Woodrow Wyatt at Connock . . . Wills, Rootes – the list of neighbours can be extended indefinitely.

Of course, the rich have to live somewhere, like everybody else, and none of these amiable gentlemen has ever done me the slightest harm. It is not their fault that they are followed by ambitious young merchant bankers, starry-eyed at the thought that if all the pound notes these men represent were put together, they would cover the whole of Wiltshire and Berkshire besides.

As it is, something profoundly disgusting has happened in the countryside. Carefree and secure folk have begun to look shifty and insecure. The story is told that one tycoon recently went out for a walk with his keeper and was shown a field full of wood pigeons. 'Fine showing of partridges,' he is said to have remarked. No doubt the story is apocryphal, but if it isn't, I know exactly what he meant. When every pigeon becomes a partridge and every goose becomes a swan, it is surely time to move.

Another advantage of the move is that we shall be surrounded by a tribe of uncles and aunties.

*   *   *

The tragic murder of the three French tourists in a Cheshire beauty spot will have lasting repercussions in the West Country. I have often noticed the wistful way in which farmers of Devon and Somerset discuss the Dominici case. When Sir Jack Drummond, his wife and daughter were brutally murdered on a camping holiday in France, one result was a sharp decline in the number of English families who took camping holidays in France. Instead, they all decided to flock to the West Country, pitching their tents, lighting their fires and digging their little lavatories by the side of the road.

Around Minehead and Glastonbury, holidaymakers from Birmingham and the industrial West Midlands have been accustomed to treat the countryside as if it were a mixture between a free hotel and a public lavatory. The wonder is that more of them have not come to a sticky end, because West Country farmers can be the most violent and unpredictable people, with a drop of cider in them, when the moon is full.

After the M5 is built, between Birmingham and Exeter, the swarms will plainly increase. Perhaps, with the tragic fate of these young French holiday-makers in mind, they will prefer to stay the night in hotels and lodging houses, which are plentiful and cheap.

*   *   *

On the whole, the West Country is taking the challenge – threat, opportunity, what you will – of the Common Market quite calmly. It is thought that the frogs of Sedgemoor might make a useful boost to exports. If, however, the pundits are right, and the whole thing is a racket to feather-bed French farmers, it seems to me that the only sane response is to become a French farmer, and this is accordingly what I have done, buying a small farm in the little-known region of Southern France called the Aude.

Next week I start moving my family into it (the animals can't follow, for fear they should catch disgusting foreign diseases). I shall then write again from the depths of the French countryside. If, as seems inevitable, more and more Englishmen decide to join the Common Market budget at the receiving end and become French farmers, my dispatches should prove a useful textbook on the various hazards and rewards to be expected.

Baby farming — and a gold medal

La Pomarede, Aude.

Journeying through the Dordogne is highly dangerous at this time of year. Hampstead intellectuals may be hiding behind every bush. Knock on any cottage door in the night, and you will be met by a furious bearded face which will explain that it is expecting Ben Whitaker for dinner, or that you have dragged it from reading the latest novel by Nicholas Mosley or Doris Lessing. It will then proceed to bore the pants off you about the iniquitous regime in Greece. The great thing is to motor through without stopping.

Apart from these people, France is still drastically under-populated. De Gaulle's policy of offering fantastic bribes to anyone who will have a baby has been continued by his successor. The friend with whom I am staying before we move into our farm has only five children, but he pays no income tax at all on his salary as a Commander in the French navy; he receives nearly £11 a week as his normal, tax-free family allowance; if he or any member of his family travels by train, bus or underground, they pay only half the fare – although, in fact, they drive a huge, white Mercedes like some African dictator on the proceeds of their family allowances, so this last concession is rather academic.

Even a four-child family like mine would receive nearly £9 a week in family allowances and travel anywhere at half-price – plus a down-payment of £105 on each baby, with a gold medal for the tenth thrown in, and with it, the privilege of asking the President of the Republic to be its godfather.

What an example this is to our own wretched Prime Minister who – whether out of meanness or out of a one-man birth limitation campaign – now refuses all requests to be a godfather, even from members of his own Cabinet; and this despite his Common Market pretensions. Perhaps the discrepancy will sort itself out when parents of large families take the logical step of emigrating to France once we join the Common Market. Even now, the prospects for anyone

prepared to surrender his British nationality and settle down to a strenuous life of baby-farming are none too bad. But English citizens who want to cash in at the receiving end of the Common Agricultural Policy by becoming French farmers have several obstacles to overcome. First, you must ask the Treasury's permission to buy a property abroad.

This is always granted but they like you to ask. Next, you must pay a premium of about quarter the purchase price as a sort of Danegeld to the Chancellor of the Exchequer, although it is hard to see quite what Mr Barber has done to deserve it apart from being born half Danish.

This extortion is particularly galling for a writer who earns most of his income abroad. First, he must bring his earnings back to England for Mr Barber to convert into his inflated, nearly worthless little green pound notes; then he must surrender nearly half of them to be redistributed however Mr Barber fancies; finally, if he wants to take any of what is left out of the country again, he must pay Mr Barber's Danegeld of twenty-five per cent. And, in case any Englishman is liable to forget who is the boss, he must send Mr Barber an annual explanation of every penny paid in or taken out of a foreign bank account. This, I suppose, is one of those freedoms which are every Englishman's birthright.

If Mr Barber would like to come and inspect our clothes before we send them to the laundry, to make sure they are well and truly dirty, I promise to stand to attention and sing Land of Hope and Glory while he does it.

In contrast to the British bureaucracy, which administers draconian and intolerable laws with a quiet efficiency and common sense, the French bureaucracy, administers equally unpleasant laws with a ferocity which is only slightly mitigated by its inefficiency.

On top of an inability to answer any letter in less than three months – then it is merely acknowledged, without any mention of the points raised – there is an obvious delight in making things as difficult as possible. The only hope is to cultivate an attitude of not caring when they tell you that you can't do something which you have already done six months before. French bureaucracy can be endlessly helpful and friendly once it has accepted that you aren't worried.

And French laws are remarkably free and easy, in other respects, like the siting of lavatories and sewage disposal. Lavatories may be sited anywhere except actually inside the kitchen, where they must be protected by a partition. Our farm was equipped with water and electricity – paid for by the Common Market Agricultural Fund – but no lavatory.

Goodness knows what the people who have been living on the spot for the last five hundred years did about this – there is not even a hole in the ground by way of a clue, and the nearest house is more than a mile away.

But there used to be a well, very deep and probably dug by the Romans which supplied the farm with water before the glorious Common Market brought us mains service. This well is the sort of thing which would become a shrine for miles around in Britain. Culture fanatics would come by the charabanc load for the pleasure of dropping money down it. Over here, it was assumed that we would want to use it for our drains, now that it has outlived its original purpose. I wouldn't want to discourage anyone from dropping money down it, but I doubt whether many wishes will be granted now.

The main crop in this region is sunflowers, which are used for vegetable oil in cooking. They make a very pretty sight at this time of year, but cultivation seemed a little strenuous to me, so we have decided to settle for fruit trees. We do not qualify for direct grants from the Common Market Agricultural Fund, which is administered locally by a very powerful and very benign organisation called SAFER, because direct help is only given to farms of twenty-one hectares or more.

It is no good asking how big a hectare is, since this is the sort of thing we argue about every day of the week. No doubt, Mr Rippon had some pretty sharp things to say about the size of these so-called hectares during the Brussels negotiations, but I know that our farm is nowhere near qualifying, and this seems to me extremely unjust. The British idea of justice means that help should be given to those who need it most, does it not? I shall be writing to my MP.

By then, of course, British housewives will be making an enormous contribution to the Agricultural Fund, and I really don't see why President Pompidou shouldn't supply us with a marble swimming bath. You begin to learn your rights when you live in France.

Whatever the Common Market may do to Britain, life in this corner of it is by no means disagreeable. Although meat is still more expensive than it is at home, there is little difference in òther food prices now, and since meat has always been more expensive here it means they take a lot of trouble in the cooking of it.

At this time of year, sweet red melons cost less than $12\frac{1}{2}$p each, and peaches are rather cheaper than eggs at about 5p a pound. The season lasts only a few weeks, but all the year round cigarettes can be bought at 11p for twenty and spirits at £1.20 a bottle. The cheapest way to be drunk is a bottle of wine at 15p, but farmers are still allowed to cook up their own spirits on a still, although they are rationed in quantity nowadays, and not allowed to sell it.

Can anyone see that happening in Britain?

The joy of life in France is that whereas necessities are rather expensive, luxuries are extremely cheap. With the peculiar genius that British politicians have for getting us the worst of every bargain, we will probably end up with our food as expensive as it is in France and our luxuries (drink and tobacco) as expensive as they already are in Britain.

We drink from mustard-pots
while the enemy creeps closer

La Pesegado, Montmaur, Aude.
Britain's Great Debate on the Common Market was followed
here with quiet incomprehension. While the fields groan and
clink with money around us, nobody can imagine a single
reason for wishing to remain outside. Wilson is seen as a
cynical villain, Mr Jenkins as the noblest Welshman of them
all. Nobody quite knows what to make of Mr Heath, or
L'Epicier, as he is called for some inexplicable reason in this
dim and distant corner of southern France.

At any rate the Great Debate was conducted in La
Pomarede, Aude, with rather more vigour and wit than
it was conducted at Westminster, to judge from newspaper
reports. Installed at last in the semi-collapsed barn two miles
from anywhere which passes for a farmhouse, we have begun
to discover some opposition to our brave venture of beating
the politicians and joining the Common Market at the
receiving end as French farmers.

The main opposition comes from a colony of French
spiders. Some are only the size of kittens, others grow to
frolic around like spaniel puppies. If one turns one's back
on them for half an hour one feels they will come bounding
out as large and as frisky as Shetland ponies. So long as they
are smaller than me and I have a stick while they have not
I think I can hold out against them, but my children are
demented by cowardice. It is lucky in many ways that
Britain no longer has an Empire to keep in order, as I do not
feel that the younger generation would be up to it.

Instead, they spend most of the day in the scorching heat

out of doors, hunting for snails. Soon, we will have to make the decision whether to eat them or not. My wife, who will be expected to cook them, feels we may be in danger of taking the Common Market challenge too seriously. Treatment involves starving them for twenty-four hours, parboiling them, removing them from their shells and cutting away the big intestine, putting them back in their shells and baking them in garlic butter. Incidentally, English snails are just as good. The last time we tried it, eight years ago while I was writing a book in the neighbourhood, they escaped and crawled all over my manuscript.

The children, of course, become very indignant at any suggestion that we should eat snails, regarding them as pets. The scandal is that even in France you can't eat spiders.

The French are brave enough to eat them, if they thought there was the slightest hope of an agreeable experience. No doubt they sometimes try to eat spiders, spitting them out with many Gallic expressions of disgust when they find that the taste has not changed. Whatever else may be said about the French, they are not cowards. During the Common Market debate, someone said that we couldn't trust them because at the battle of the Somme we had lost a million men after the French mutinied in the face of the enemy.

23

In my newspaper, this remark was attributed, surprisingly, to Mr Reginald Paget, the Labour MP for Northampton. If Mr Paget really said that, we can only suppose it is true, since he is one of the very few MPs who add lustre to that dismal institution. But if true, it is rather sad, since there is a general feeling in France that the Great War marked one of those rare episodes in French history when everybody behaved rather well, what with the taxis of the Marne and so on.

They are indeed a most complicated race. If the charming and beautiful Southerners we have landed among are kinder and more hospitable than their northern neighbours, they are certainly no less complicated. You hear no false heroics about the Resistance down here for the good reason that there was no resistance, although all the village war memorials of 1939-45 carry longer lists of the dead for the last years of the war than for the first years, before the surrender.

These are the Frenchmen who were killed in Russia and the Ukraine, fighting with the Germans against the Red Army. They were volunteers in the cruellest and bitterest campaign of modern history. Goodness knows why they volunteered.

There is no suggestion that they were coerced, but few could have been highly educated or highly political. Perhaps if they had been better educated they would have known about Napoleon's retreat from Moscow and stayed at home; but there is no reason to be sure of this as French education, though tough, is highly selective where French history is concerned. In any case, whatever decided these sons of the soil that Stalin was marginally worse than Hitler, whatever drove them to fight it out in the freezing cold of Stalingrad, it certainly wasn't cowardice.

My own family is engaged in a campaign of similar bitterness and intensity at the moment. Although we brought most of the furniture and utensils from Wiltshire, we stupidly forgot to bring any glasses. The Bank of England explains very clearly that although Mr Barber allows you to buy food with your travel allowance (thank you very much, Sir) you are not allowed to buy furniture or household utensils. Glasses are household utensils. For these, you must spend investment dollars, bought at a premium of twenty-five per cent. But you are allowed to buy food! How wonderful to be an Englishman and enjoy these heady freedoms.

There is a firm of mustard manufacturers in France whose mustard is rather nasty, but who have had the clever idea of putting it into pots which when washed out become drinking glasses. The glass we are engaged on now has a tasteful picture of Babar, King of the Elephants, and Queen Celeste. The next one promises a representation of Snow White, with at least three of her seven dwarfs. By the time we have finished seven pots of this really most unpleasant mustard, we will have a glass each, not allowing for breakages.

Quite apart from a fixed determination not to give Mr Barber a penny more of our hard-earned money than we need, we find our supply of investment dollars dwindling. But one begins to understand how these Frenchmen from the Lauragais must have felt, fighting another country's war and starving to death in twenty feet of snow, four thousand miles from home.

Of course, this is not an entirely accurate picture of life at La Pesegado. The heat is so intense that it makes you gasp whenever you set foot outside, and food is dangerously abundant. The name of La Pesegado is *patois* for a place where mud is weighed. Apparently the inhabitants of my farm spent all their time in this diverting and harmless occupation, before the French Revolution came, destroying all idea of harmony, social order and traditional values. Nowadays, there is not even any mud around, so one could not weigh it even if one had the time, inclination and necessary machinery.

The ancient *patois* of Languedoc survives among the older peasants. This means that they can communicate only with each other, since no Frenchman understands them, and they understand no French. It solves the generation gap in the most marvellous way, and to everybody's complete satisfaction.

The few old-timers who are sufficiently evolved to have learned a little French seldom have anything very interesting to say, in my experience, and no doubt my conversation bores them as much as theirs bores me. With monoglot *patois* speakers, we merely exchange smiles of exaggerated delight before going our separate ways, fortified by a general feeling of benevolence.

What a good idea it would be if British teachers, instead of filling their pupils' heads with a lot of boring, out-dated rubbish about contraception, abortion, and how to masturbate, could teach each generation an entirely different language. Only those who wish to promote strife for their own sinister purposes can seriously pretend that there is anything to be gained at this stage of our nation's history by the generations talking to each other.

Perhaps this is building too much on the fact that my children are being very tiresome about spiders, that they seem to have lost entirely the quality which once made Britain great.

Le Fat's reward — our great snail collection

La Pesegado, Montmaur, Aude.
A lorry carrying 100,000 eggs crashed near here and every egg was broken. As soon as we heard the news, we piled into the car, reckoning that one does not have the opportunity to see 100,000 broken eggs twice in a lifetime, but we were two days late and the mess had been cleared up. This is most unusual in France, where the main roads are littered with crashed and burned-out vehicles like the Sinai Desert.

In the Army I shared a barrack-room with someone who was concerned about the decline of religion in England. The trouble was that nobody any longer had an awareness of Death, he said, as we spat on our boots into the small hours, because dead and dying people were always whisked away before any survivor had time to reflect on the frailty of the human condition and so on. He would be much happier in France.

Last week, my wife arrived at the scene of an accident in Toulouse. Twenty-five minutes later the injured were still lying on the ground while bystanders conducted an acrimonious debate about which of the unconscious figures was more to blame. Next day, we went to the sea at Leucate, where a young woman collapsed in the water. She was fished out and left on the sand unconscious for three-quarters of an hour while a Grand Debate was held on the subject of what was wrong with her and whether it justified the enormous expense of an ambulance. Eventually, she was bundled into a car, still unconscious, and driven away.

In France, there is a law which obliges people to save

fellow-citizens' lives under penalty of a heavy fine. My French friends listen wide-eyed when I tell them that in England it is left to the discretion of the individual whether to save a drowning man or not. Perhaps the crowd in Toulouse was arguing about who would have to pay the fine if nobody telephoned an ambulance.

The great Waugh snail collection has come to its appointed sticky end. One day after a rainstorm we collected nearly a hundred really fat ones in just over an hour. My wife mutinied and refused to cook them. Eventually, we gave them to a man known as Fat François, or more simply Le Fat, as a reward for plastering and rewiring the entire house.

This François is quite easily the fattest man I have ever seen outside a circus, and also the most dignified. Normally, he works the fields for a neighbouring farmer, but he is also an expert carpenter, electrician, plumber, plasterer, glass-cutter and everything else. As head of the family, he earns £15 a week, which would probably not do for you or me, but he also has a free house and free farm produce, including wine. He personally drinks four litres of wine a day, and is never noticeably either worse or better for it. He works very hard indeed, with a mere two hours off for lunch, and is the only man I have ever seen standing literally in a pool of his own sweat, when he helped plaster a ceiling on a hot day.

After work he picks bunches of wild lavender which grows around the house, explaining that he likes to have wild lavender in his underwear drawer. Recently his wife suffered some form of a nervous breakdown, a very rare complaint in these parts. When I asked him how she was getting on, he replied : 'She is completely deranged. At breakfast today, I had to ask her three times before she passed the cheese.' A normal breakfast for the working man of these parts is cassoulet, made out of white beans, lean pork, sausage, skin of pork and garlic. The cowman of a neighbour, describing to his employer how extremely ill he had been the day before, explained that he had found it necessary to push this mixture down his throat at breakfast with his finger, because he was unable to swallow.

There can be no doubt that Le Fat earned his snails, and his noises of pleasure when they were presented must mean that they have found a happy home. My children have now given up snail hunting in favour of wild flowers, so my desk is like an illustration from Mr Keble-Martin's masterpiece, even if it has not yet earned itself a foreword by Prince Philip.

The desk is tucked away in a barn, already part-occupied by last year's straw, part by this year's hay. One puts up with the discomfort more easily now because at last, two weeks after moving in, we have managed to finish buying the property. The man who did this for us was Maître Belloc, the local notary. He is a handsome devil, with side-whiskers and a reckless suntan. He was puzzled that my wife should be the owner of La Pesegado, explaining that in France these things are settled by a marriage contract which determines exactly who owns what and usually ends in joint ownership. He was tickled to learn of our appalling English libel laws, which mean that no English writer who takes the business seriously can own anything, and seemed more attentive than ever to my dear wife after these revelations.

I did not tell him that we may also be most grateful for

a foreign bolt-hole now that Britain has started sending her writers to prison. My last days in London were spent almost entirely at the Old Bailey for the Oz trial. It seemed the best entertainment in London at the time, although I was disconcerted by the way the Chief Treasury Counsel, Mr Brian Leary, kept winking at me as I sat on the Press Bench. I am almost sure we have never been introduced.

Richard Neville seemed brave, sincere and highly articulate. If he can escape from prison disguised as a washerwoman I shall be delighted to give him and his friends sanctuary here for as long as they like. They can try smoking some of last year's straw, if they wish, and see if it gives them any vibrations, or whatever.

Straw disposal is in fact, one of the major hazards of the neighbourhood. Far more is produced than anyone can use for bedding animals, so the only thing is to burn it. This is extremely dangerous in an area where the smallest spark can cause a major conflagration, and is, in fact, illegal unless the mayor of the village is told in advance, and unless one has three fire fighters at hand. Nobody pays the slightest attention to these rules, and I have never heard of a mayor objecting.

Mayors are elected on a six-year basis, and have almost unlimited power during their term of office. They can imprison rioters, summon the militia and even call the citizens to arms if this seems a useful or desirable thing to do. I shall probably be writing again about mayors, since they determine, among other things, which houses shall be provided with hard roads by the council. As our house is surrounded on every side by about two miles of cart track, I think I may have to put myself up for election as mayor, which is the usual method of getting things done in the French countryside.

But it seems a most unsatisfactory state of affairs when fatuous laws are passed, as they increasingly are – like Mrs Castle's vehicle specifications – to which nobody pays the slightest attention until those in authority decide to make an example of a particular person. In France, Richard Neville would probably have risked having the militia called out against him on several occasions, but the risk seems worth taking when one contemplates the havoc which can be caused in England nowadays by one policeman with a toothache or one Treasury Counsel with a twitch in his eye.

Pity the poor French rich

La Pesegado, Montmaur, Aude.
I never thought that I would live to see a Frenchman put tomato ketchup on his beefsteak. Sad to say, ketchup has taken the Midi by storm. Barbecue parties are given every night which might more properly be called ketchup parties,

where guests smother their food and themselves with the stuff until they resemble film extras in some particularly grisly Hammer Studios production. Mercifully, they have not learned about ketchup sandwiches yet.

The hospitality of the area is stupendous. Most nights, it seems, we sit quaffing the ketchup until two o'clock in the morning. Within a largish circle of local landowners, all cousins of each other or old friends, somebody gives a party nearly every evening. Above a certain age, they sit playing bridge all day and all night. Under that age, they amuse themselves as best they can until reaching the bridge age.

Landowners have left the heavily fortified castles which dominate every village in the neighbourhood. From them, their ancestors used to wage religious wars of unbelievable ferocity. Nowadays, these castles are either empty or bought by doctors and professional people from Toulouse, who use them as holiday homes.

The Château de Montmaur was bought last year by a professional man for under £8,000. It has about thirty vast rooms, complete with fifteenth-century fireplaces, turrets, spiral staircases, but would need about £120,000 spent on it to bring it anywhere near the standard of comfort of a modern council house.

The laws of inheritance are very strange in France, and it is a mystery how the rich survive. French couples are bound by law to leave their property equally divided among all their children, except for a quarter, which they can dispose of however they wish. Death duties are very small within the family, punitive and confiscatory outside it – almost as bad as our standard rates in England. Hence all the mysterious contracts of marriage and divisions of property which take up so much of their time, from the humblest to the richest in the land.

The final result seems to be that a much larger number of people are comfortably off, and they all seem to have a most enjoyable time. In England, the rich always seem rather lonely, poor things, having practically nobody to share their hours of idleness with. Perhaps they feel guilty, too, having dispossessed their brothers and sisters so cruelly.

If French laws applied in Britain, Blenheim, Chatsworth, Woburn and Longleat would all be inhabited up to their rooftops by uncles, aunts and cousins, each with his inalienable right to an apartment. And a very good thing, too.

Another result of the French law on inheritance is that the family is much more closely knit than in England, because cousins all tend to live in the same neighbourhood, tied to their property. Members of the old nobility live for the most part in converted farmhouses, whose barns have been turned into ballrooms or ketchup centres. Village life revolves around a more or less benign nepotism, through the mayoral system, from which nearly everybody profits, since everybody is related to somebody else except for the Algerians. Consequently, the village survives as a social and cultural unit to an extent which must be rare in the modern world outside Africa.

At this time of year, every village holds its three-day fête. It would be polite to describe these events in terms of a courting ritual, and this was certainly their old function, but nowadays, I fear, they are only used for mating purposes.

Even in the smallest villages, three bands may be hired. People dance in the village square for three days and two nights – not Morris dances and dainty, old-tyme quick steps, but a curious, shuffling bear-hug. The bands are not always very good, and the funniest moment is usually when they turn up to play in church on the Sunday morning. Afterwards, they play the Last Post and the Marseillaise in front of the village war memorial, which I am afraid is equally funny. This is the one day of the year when the men go to church, looking very respectable in black berets and smelling like badgers after two days and nights of dissipation.

The Aude was in the centre of the religious wars which tore France apart for centuries. Catholics and Protestants massacred each other in every village sometimes throwing each other off great heights, sometimes burning each other alive. Nowadays, everybody seems to have lost interest.

The Catholic church in the Midi bears a striking resemblance to our own beloved Church of England. In the few villages where there is still a priest, his congregation is usually two old peasant women, both deaf, toothless and heavily whiskered, who pay not the smallest attention to his daring new doctrines and latest eye-catching gimmicks, as he performs alone in the dripping gloom at the other end of the church.

Village fêtes in the French manner would never work in England, of course. This is partly because our country villages are mostly inhabited by retired people, who have no particular use for mating rituals and would resent the noise. It is also partly because they would always be broken up by gangs of toughs from the nearest big town. Strangely enough, there is very little of this sort of violence under the surface of French life, at any rate in the country. This may be because the family unit is so much stronger; young people have a recognised place in society and do not need to form gangs for their own protection. It may be because village solidarity is greater and villagers more assertive in France. In my own village of Combe Florey in Somerset, hooligans from Bridgwater broke every window in the village street one night a few years ago. Not a single person turned on a light, let alone went out to remonstrate with them.

But my own explanation for the impossibility of having such village fêtes is the same as it is for nearly all the social and political ills of England, from industrial disputes to the sexual gaucherie of the average English male. This is the murderous and catastrophic price of drink.

The local newspaper gives far more coverage to events in Northern Ireland than it does to anything which may be happening in Paris. This may be because religious wars were once big news down here, in the thirteenth, fifteenth and sixteenth centuries. But the people most interested are the *pieds noirs* or Algerian settlers, whose "Algerie Française" campaign bears so much resemblance to the insistence of English and Scots settlers that Northern Ireland is part of Britain.

A million and a quarter *pieds noirs* have resettled themselves in France over the last ten years mostly in the south around me. They cannot see why "loyalist" Northern Irishmen should not resettle themselves in England, any more than they can understand all the fuss about East African Asians. Although these *pieds noirs* are not exactly coloured, few of them would stand much chance of being chosen as models for a soap advertisement. Their resettlement has been almost painless, although, of course, France is a much bigger country than Britain, and much less densely populated. But the psychological difference is even greater.

France sees her inhabitants as assets, people who add to the wealth and importance of the country, whereas Britain, I think, tends to see them as liabilities – people who must somehow be housed, medicated, pensioned, imprisoned, educated and adequately drained at the public expense. Far better let the Ulstermen all settle in Rhodesia, where their magnificent loyalty to the Crown will come in useful.

The curious case of the hirsute hermit

La Pesegado, Montmaur, Aude.

So many people who choose to live in the country are accused of being hermits that it is quite interesting to meet my first genuine hermit – rather like the occasion in London when I was able to introduce a Jesuit to a man who thought he was Jesus Christ. 'A member of your Society, sir,' I muttered at the time.

Abbé Blanchard lives completely alone with a dog in his hermitage a few miles outside the wine-producing village of Fitou, in the Corbières. Every morning he says Mass and then has the rest of the day to himself. In appearance he would probably be taken for some ex-editor of *Oz* in retirement, with long white hair and flowing beard.

His conversation is predictably crazy, all about the Emperor Charlemagne and various sacred lines on which the crusaders built their chapels. True, in place of a hermit's black garb he wears a blue T-shirt with jeans and I found him suspiciously plump for someone who should be on a diet of wild honey and locusts. But he must have had some sort of aura about him, because my children forbore from what I should have thought would be the irresistible temptation to pull his beard.

We found him on a tour of the Corbières. Every vineyard in the area gives free wine tastings to anyone who turns up. You probably spend more on petrol than the value of the wine – the price of petrol is one of the major scandals of French public life – but it is quite a pleasant way of passing the time, nevertheless.

Fitou, as it happens, is locally renowned for its wine, although little thought of outside the region. On a small country lane which leads to Fitou from Treilles, another wine-producing village in the hills above the Mediterranean, there is a handwritten signpost pointing along a track in the wilderness to the ancient chapel of St Aubin.

At this point I became absurdly over-excited, thinking that it said St Auberon. If ever there was a St Auberon, he is so little known and so little revered that the Vatican has not even bothered to deny his existence. But the crazy hermit seemed to think that there was a St Aubin, Archbishop of Embrun, in the Alps, who died around 650.

Perhaps he is right in thinking that there was once a hermitage, leper hospital and chapel of the eighth century on the spot. He claims to have found a few arches when he arrived to support this theory, but what stands today was almost entirely built by himself and he can plainly call it whatever he likes.

Having failed to establish the cult of St Auberon, I determined to discover why the hermit looked so well-fed. Was he brought loaves of bread every day by the ravens, like St Benedict? Inquiries in the village of Fitou revealed the existence of a rich patron, a marquise, who is so taken with his holy life that the two are often to be seen together in restaurants, eating gigantic four-course meals and discussing the Emperor Charlemagne animatedly. I have often noticed

that one of the consolations of the religious life is the admiration it excites among womenfolk.

This solved the puzzle of the corpulent hermit, but I should like to think that it would not be too difficult to live off the land, if there were no marquises around to help out. On the farm where we buy our melons – beautiful sweet orange ones for 7p each – the farmer collects two tons of them every morning out of a four-acre field, and, according to his beautiful daughter, will continue to do so from the middle of August until the first week of October. Nearly everybody keeps rabbits in hutches to eat, which breed like my co-religionists in Belfast and cost nothing to feed. I wonder why so few people keep them in England, except as pets.

Unfortunately, there are no wild rabbits to eat at present. Another wave of myxomatosis has hit the neighbourhood, and wherever one goes by day or by night one sees the dazed, stricken creatures waiting to die. The sight sickens and infuriates me as much as others are sickened and infuriated by South Africa, the Greek Colonels, Mr Peregrine Worsthorne or Mr Harold Wilson. A speaker in the House of Lords recently urged that penalties for deliberately spreading myxomatosis should be removed on the grounds that the law was widely disregarded and the disease was beneficial to the human race. A much better idea would surely be to reintroduce the old English punishment of village stocks. Of course, there would be no shortage of people urging the reintroduction of stocks for stag-hunting, an occupation which has always seemed to me sensible and useful in working off some of the cruder emotions of my Somerset neighbours, as well as picturesque.

My next-door neighbour, but one, at La Pesegado is a farmer who spends his entire day watching his cows as they graze. He has only thirteen of them, and sometimes he speaks to them in a high-pitched, angry voice, always in *patois*. Recently, he introduced them to me very formally, one by one : Frissoni, Blanchette, Rosalie, Trompette, Margot, Grisette, Fanje . . . When it rains, he sits watching them from a Citroen Deux Chevaux parked in a corner of the field. That is what the Common Market has done for French agriculture. Like the hermit who lives alone with his dog, this angry old man who spends the day denouncing his cows in *patois* seems to have discovered what country life is all about.

This is borne out by a discovery I have made about the Languedoc *patois* – that it is almost completely meaningless. In an earlier dispatch, I said that the name of this house – La Pesegado – derived from the *patois* name for a place where mud is weighed. The Mayor of Montmaur, however, claims that the name derives from its alternative meaning of a footprint. There used to be a huge stone on the track outside the farm – he had seen it often – which showed the impression of a foot, with toes clearly marked. Legend had it that this was the footprint of an angel who landed on the hillside many centuries ago. Then, in 1940, the farmer who owned the place grew fed up with having an angel's footprint on his doorstep and broke the stone to pieces.

This story illustrates not only the robust attitude of the countryside to ancient monuments and angels, but also the amazing ambiguity of the Languedoc language. Goodness knows what other meanings the word has, but if *patois* speakers can never be sure whether they are talking about an angel's footprint or a place for weighing mud it scarcely seems worth the effort to make conversation.

Having seen the general direction which a rustic, secluded life down here can be expected to take, I think it is time to return to England and start worrying about poor Mr Heath again. Perhaps he needs a long and serious conversation with one of my cows down here. Blanchette is the most communicative.

Well I'm *pleased our pub can keep its thatch*

Chilton Foliat, Wiltshire.

Our village has just witnessed a great victory for the forces of truth and beauty against those of greed and indifference. An inspector sent from Mr Peter Walker's Department of the Environment has rejected the brewers' appeal to replace the thatched roof of our village pub with tiles. Unless the Secre-

tary of State makes one of his lightning interventions, it looks as if the brewers have been beaten, for once.

There are those who sometimes suggest that ministerial decisions are influenced by the very large contributions which many brewery firms make to the Conservative Party. We should all be grateful to the brewers for the selfless way they help to keep democracy alive in this country, but I think it would be quite wrong to suppose that my old friend Peter Walker allows gratitude of this sort to override his very genuine concern for favourable personal publicity.

I should like to report that the inspector's decision was greeted by scenes of wild festivity in Chilton Foliat – dancing in the streets, fountains running with cider, whole oxen roasted on spits. My earlier dispatches on this issue might have unwittingly given the impression of something like a second Peasants' Revolt on its way. Certainly, I was not at all surprised to learn that a few key Cabinet Ministers had doubled their bodyguard. Soon, we would have learned of machine-gun emplacements set up around the Grocery in Downing Street, of Peter Walker accompanied wherever he went by a mounted troop of Life Guards in full ceremonial dress. But the sad truth is that inspector's courageous and wise decision passed almost unnoticed in the village, except among a small handful of middle-class busybodies who hardly ever go into the pub, for fear of boredom. Those honest folk who do use it would not mind if it had a roof of corrugated iron so long as it had a roof.

It is just a lonely certainly that we are right and everybody else wrong, which makes it worthwhile for us busybodies to go on making a nuisance of ourselves. Our job is to keep both the simple Philistines and the greedy rich in their places, to prevent them, in their stupidity and avarice, from destroying everything that is left.

Mr Khrushchev is a typical example of a simple Philistine who was never kept in his place. To read the obituary notices of this jolly, liberal-minded peasant, one might almost forget that he had personally supervised the murder and deportation of some million and a half of his fellow-countrymen – in Moscow, during the pre-war purges, and later in the Ukraine – before even coming to power and sending the tanks into Hungary.

There is a man I know of who has grown his hair down to his waist, for some reason. He makes a most engaging sight as he drives by, hair streaming behind him like Botticelli's Venus.

Quite possibly he would prove a fund of earthy humour and peasant shrewdness if I engaged him in conversation; he might teach me how to rap the table with my shoes and score a debating point. I wish him nothing but success and prosperity in his chosen profession of tractor driver. But I sometimes wonder as I watch him drive past just how many Englishmen he would find it necessary to murder and deport if we made him First Secretary of the Western Region, in charge of all local government in the West of England.

I also think the days of his Botticelli hairstyle may be numbered with the arrival of the 'super-louse'. This animal has been identified by Mr John Maunder, of the London School of Hygiene and Tropical Medicine. It is resistant to DDT and other common insecticides, and has apparently established itself in the hair of a million British children already. Perhaps there is a new generation of skinheads on the way.

*   *   *

Before we left for France, I put a large bowl of rat poison in an attic above the bedroom I share with my wife. Seven weeks later, I find that the poison has all been eaten, but far from hurting the mice it appears to have had the effect of a fertility drug and mild euphoriant. They now stamp and crash above our heads every night, making the sort of noise one would expect from a platoon of Welsh Guardsmen on Ladies' Night. I resent this much less than my dear wife. It is not just that I don't mind mice, but I have always rather liked them.

It is the gentler sex which drives mankind into this cruel vendetta against mice. Rats, of course, are quite different and utterly horrible. Whenever I used to see them swarm out of a cornrick at threshing time, I was reminded of Londoners in the rush-hour. Perhaps rats are full of Cockney wit and liberated sexual behaviour when you get to know them, but, like Londoners I feel they are best kept at a distance. Moreover, they are used to justify man's genocidal campaign against mice.

Perhaps women can perceive a terrifying affinity between themselves and these gentlest of creatures. This would explain their animosity. Like most people, I try to keep an open mind about the Women's Liberation Movement, as about all the other exciting and wonderful things that are happening in the modern world. As soon as its leaders can show me a race of women who do not scream and climb up the wall every time they see a mouse, I might even start taking them seriously. Until then, I can only appeal to members of my own sex – most especially to thoughtful, humane Englishmen of the middle class – not to be stampeded into taking sides in something which is not, fundamentally, their quarrel.

Morals slip as the M4 marches on

Chilton Foliat, Wiltshire.

Down here, we sorely missed London's great Festival of Light, when the Underground trains were apparently full of young people singing 'Onward Christian Soldiers'. This is exactly what has always been needed. Travel on the Underground, always one of the most boring and disgusting things in London, is shortly to become one of the most expensive. A little community singing is obviously the answer. In my

London days I had an uneasy feeling that if I started up all alone, nobody else would join in. Perhaps some good Christian society like the MRA or the CIA might supply hymn books in every compartment and then, in the new glow which Lord Longford has kindled, it might be worth trying.

Our own attempt at a Festival of Light in Wiltshire some time ago was not a great success. Appalled by the moral pollution and so on of the normal run of our acquaintances,

we asked a venerable American priest to dinner with a sexagenarian cousin who happened to be visiting the country. The
sexagenarian fell asleep very early in the evening, and
we decided not to wake him, as he had had a very good
war.

The American priest, however, became hopelessly over-
excited and confused as the evening progressed. At the end of
the meal we produced an Apple Charlotte which the priest ate
with many noises of appreciation. 'Ma'am,' he said, 'these are
the best potatoes I have ever eaten.' Half an hour later my
dear wife said she was feeling unwell and went to bed, where
she developed mumps in the night.

There is no room for complacency about the general state
of morality even in Wiltshire, I am sorry to say. My spiciest
stories on this subject must wait until we finally leave the
neighbourhood at the end of next month.

The outbreak of cattle rustling near Lambourn is generally
attributed to construction of the M4 motorway. Similar stories
are still being told about the building of the Great Western
Railway, which brought gangs of drunken and licentious Irishmen into the heart of the West Country.

At least the M4 workers are extremely rich while their job
lasts – many, being self-employed, take home as much as £80
a week for shifting earth. Just as anybody who has ever been
into a pub will know that it is better to be stuck with a rich
bore than with a poor bore, so if a maiden has been despoiled
on the M4 she can comfort herself that she has sold her virtue
dear. But with the best will in the world, it is hard to see why
anybody decided that building this particular motorway was
worth the risk to local morals. It must be part of the modern
age's insane passion for moving things.

When in Somerset we live only six miles from the sea, but
all our fish has to come from Billingsgate. There is a slaughter-
house only nine miles away, but all the meat comes from
Smithfied. Goods are rushed through our beautiful countryside between identical conurbations for no reason except to
create movement.

A lorry driver I met recently was driving an extremely commonplace cargo between Swindon and London. When I urged him to take it back to Swindon, since it could not make the slightest difference which town it was in, he said that he was prevented from doing this by a sense of duty to his employers. But if I wanted to steal the lorry and cargo, he said, he would let me do so in exchange for a quarter of the proceeds.

He, too, was a victim of moral pollution, poor man – probably influenced by all these strip clubs and Chinese restaurants which are springing up everywhere.

If countryfolk miss wholesome entertainments like Lord Longford's Festival of Light, they also miss all the worry about unemployment. Whatever the unemployed may have had to suffer in the north during the thirties, down here nowadays they live a dignified and settled existence. Many have been living on supplementary benefit for eight years or more. One of these assured me at the last election that he did not intend to vote because the Government had never done anything for him. He would certainly take a very dim view of any politician who pushed him into a job just to get the national average down.

One old man comes and sits under a tree to eat a tube of Smarties every morning. Then he throws the empty tube over the wall into my garden and goes home. These empty tubes are collected by my children, who have a variety of uses for them, and in this way the old man makes a genuine contribution to the sum of human happiness in the world.

If he worked in a factory, on the other hand, he would merely add a little to the huge stockpile of unnecessary and useless objects being rushed backwards and forwards between our major cities.

It is surely one of the joys of technological capitalism that despite its noise, smell, dirt and accompanying moral pollution, it requires only about a third of our citizens to work. Everybody else can live quite happily off the excess production, leaving work to those who enjoy it, or who are greedy to

47

have more than anybody else, or whose emotional inadequacies require them to boss other people around.

In any case, I hope those who find themselves unexpectedly out of work as a result of Mr Heath's abrasive policies use the time to catch up on their reading. This month, Oxford University Press brought out a book which describes and illustrates every known British creepy-crawly. It is called the *Oxford Book of Invertebrates* and must be one of the most fascinating books on this or any other subject.

Some weeks ago I commented on the amazing fact that the French have never got around to eating spiders. According to this book, one species of spider was frequently eaten in England as a cure for the ague. This is the *Tegenaria Saeva* – the large, hairy sort you always find in the bottom of your bath. If anyone wishes to avoid prescription charges on an attack of the ague, these spiders should be fished out of the bath, 'gently bruised and wrapped up in a raisin or spread upon bread and butter'. I'll bring Mr Barber to his knees yet.

The book also reveals how they get into the bath, thus resolving the endless debate about whether they climb up the drainpipe, crawl through the overflow or drop from the ceiling. To reveal the answer would be to give too much away. Most of us may have jobs now, but there is no reason to suppose we will have them for very long, and the *Oxford Book of Invertebrates* is something to look forward to during those long hours of leisure which may be ahead.

I've been thinking a lot of the Wali of Swat . . .

Chilton Foliat, Wiltshire.
Undoubtedly the event of the fortnight, if not the decade, has
been the Chilton Foliat Primary School play: *King Arthur
and the Knights of the Round Table*. Miss Julia Hope was an
admirably relaxed King Arthur; Master Anton Henley cut a

fine figure as Merlin; Miss Sophia Waugh was a decorative
Sir Kay. But the most important thing is that a good time
was had by all. It was produced by Mr Edward Porter, the
village headmaster, with a vigour and panache which would
have been wasted in a less worthy cause.

His school is a new one, completed only a year ago at a
cost of some £25,000. It was being planned at the same time
as the Labour Government had to defer raising the school

49

leaving age, and I opposed it strongly at the time pointing out that we already had a perfectly good school, and there were more urgent priorities than a new Plasticine palace for the toddlers of Chilton Foliat. But Mr Porter's Pleasure Dome arose nevertheless, and I must now admit that in terms of the pleasure it has caused, Mr Jenkins never spent a wiser £25,000.

It is said that few people in the towns chose to indulge in amateur theatricals after leaving school. Family and village concerts were a large part of my own childhood, but they are some of the many advantages of belonging to a large family in the country. Amateur theatricals still survive in country house parties and in the Women's Institutes. One of the most enjoyable evenings I can remember was spent at a concert given by the Welford and Wickham Women's Institute near Newbury, when all the village chiefs and elders dressed up as chickens and cows and walked round the village hall clucking and mooing to the tune of 'Old MacDonald had a Farm'.

This may not be everybody's idea of fun, but at least people should give it a try. It is no good sitting in front of the television all day eating chocolate biscuits and expecting to discover happiness. Of course, such people may suffer less than audiences at amateur theatricals.

My great-grandfather, who was a general practitioner in the East Somerset village of Midsomer Norton, used to act his amateur theatricals for hours on end to the unfortunate villagers. If any of them fell asleep or ran away, he almost certainly took his revenge in the form of some particularly nasty medicine for their various appalling diseases. He was a very determined man, as well as being a very bad actor.

Urban society is in danger of forgetting that nothing is enjoyable unless it has been preceded by some shortage or discomfort. Rich people who live in the country generally understand this. After a day's hunting or shooting in the rain, one gets more pleasure out of a poached egg than anyone would get from an eight-course banquet who had spent the day in a centrally-heated room watching television and smoking cigarettes. Enjoyment must involve the cultivation of appetites.

Soon sex will be the only pleasure left for town-dwellers; eventually they will grow too lazy even for that. They will lie in a stupor, their erotic fantasies constantly interrupted by soft, seductive voices urging them to eat more chocolate biscuits.

One man who certainly has enough of the countryside around him to avoid this fate is Lord Bradford, who lives at Weston Park, in Shropshire. But, instead of getting on with his amateur theatricals, pheasant-bashing and other duties, this nobleman has taken to writing letters to *The Times* of a most violent and unpleasant nature about grey squirrels:

'The grey squirrel is an unmitigated pest . . . It is high time that the grey squirrel should be recognised for what it is, a useless and serious pest,' he splutters, urging that they should be poisoned 'as a matter of extreme urgency'.

At times, he even rises to the eloquence of an Enoch: 'This alien invader has also eliminated over most of the country that far more attractive native mammal, the red squirrel.'

I know nothing about Lord Bradford, but his house is one of the glories of Britain. I am happy to think of him enjoying the park laid out by Inigo Jones, the tapestry room, the temple by James Paine. If ever I visit the place I fully intend to offer him a sweet, but I also very much like grey squirrels.

Those of us who would defend the right of Lord Bradford to live in Weston Park, with our lives if necessary, must also accept that those grey squirrels have exactly the same right to live in his trees. I have often noticed how big landowners are tempted to avarice and jealousy. It is time Lord Bradford realised that as far as most people are concerned he and the squirrels are part of the same act, so they might as well learn to live together. If Lord Bradford does not retire from this campaign, I shall suggest that Weston Park be taken over as a hostel for immigrant families, on the grounds that immigrants are the more attractive mammals.

Talking of which I was sad to see how little attention people in Britain gave to the fact that the former Wali of Swat had died. Perhaps, like myself, most Englishmen were not even aware of his existence until reading of his untimely death last week. As soon as I read *The Times*'s obituary notice by Sir Ambrose Dundas, I realised that a light had gone out in the world :

' "The Wali" as we all knew him, was a spare, athletic creature with a commanding look and at one time zip-fasteners, for which he developed a craze, all over him.'

He was also a grandson of the Akond of Swat, about whom Edward Lear wrote the immortal poem :

> Who, or why, or which, or WHAT
> Is the Akond of Swat?

It never fails to amaze me that the Indian sub-continent has failed to catch the imagination of contemporary Englishmen, as Africa has caught it, despite the fact that only forty years ago there can scarcely have been a family in the country without some Indian connection.

At the Labour Party Conference, in Brighton, I spent a large part of the time with a beautiful lady from Bangladesh trying to interest people in the appalling, unspeakable things which are now happening in East Pakistan. Nobody was much interested, although only two people refused to join her 'Friends of Bangladesh'. One of these was a BBC employee of no consequence, who enquired with a sneer how much money we were earning for our support of the Bengali cause.

The other, I am sorry to say, was my cousin, Mr David Watt, political editor of the *Financial Times*, who declined to join the Friends of Bangladesh on the grounds that he did not know enough about the matter to have formed an opinion.

> And if he suddenly screams and wakes
> Do they bring him only a few small cakes or a LOT
> For the Akond of Swat?

The greatest joker of them all — could it be Picasso?

On the road to Combe Florey, Somerset.
At Chilton Foliat, we celebrated Picasso's ninetieth birthday with a grand bonfire of paintings and other works of art brought home by my children from school. One of the joys of moving house is that so much has to be thrown away. Perhaps their paintings will improve in Somerset, where I doubt that a single original work by Picasso is to be found.

This, in fact, is one of the reasons we are going there — to escape the various forms of madness which urban life encourages — but a well-meaning lady I met in London said that moving house itself could have a harmful effect on small children. So it seemed a sensible precaution to break the journey at Corsley, near Frome, and visit the tomb of their great-great-great-grandfather, Rev. James Hay Waugh, who

53

was Rector of Corsley for forty-one years until his death in 1885.

He spent most of his time composing inscriptions for his own tombstone and delivering sermons about his impending death: 'When this feeble voice no longer guides you,' he would say, 'when this shaking hand is at rest from its labours . . .' He lived to be nearly eighty-eight and then, after a particularly sad sermon, lay down on the floor of his study in Corsley Rectory and died.

Obviously, death is not the sort of thing to discuss at the same time as a fellow's ninetieth birthday. I have never had anything against Picasso, and certainly find his painting no worse than the things which my children do every day at school and which I am expected to greet with cries of wonder and amazement. But I have always thought it extremely odd that he should have been born so soon after a supreme comedian like P. G. Wodehouse, whose ninetieth birthday we celebrated ten days before. The whole science of astrology rests upon the proposition that human character is decided by the stars under which people are born. For Picasso to have been born so close to Wodehouse may disprove the whole theory, or it may suggest that we have all been completely wrong in our assessment of Picasso until this moment.

In all the noises of the Pseuds' Field-day which marked the event, not a single voice has suggested that Picasso is, quite simply, the greatest practical joker of all time: that he has taken on the entire fashionable, intellectual and artistic world, pulling its collective leg for the past sixty-five years. Perhaps, when he dies, a document will be found containing his last message to the world. Three words would suffice, or even less – whatever is the Spanish equivalent of *Ever been had?*

The endless torrent of pompous, boring rubbish about Picasso drove me away from the newspapers, and my last days at Chilton Foliat were spent reading letters, receipts and other family accounts of the last century. A great advantage of living in the country is that one has the space and leisure in which to cultivate one's ancestors.

Last week, however, I discovered what may be the vital clue to an unrevealed Victorian murder story. I hesitate to reveal it now, since it involves not only my own great-grandfather in the role of murderer, but also the great-grandfather of a much-loved man in public life, the wise and temperate editor of a national newspaper, in the role of murderee.

The clue itself is a five-page bill from Messrs Rees-Mogg and Davy, solicitors, of Cholwell, to my great-grandfather Dr Alexander Waugh, of Midsomer Norton, dated 1889. Rees-Mogg and Davy had advised him in a slander case against someone called Mr George Carter. Carter, they said, had put it around that 'if certain persons at Clandown refused to vote for a certain candidate for the Office of County Councillor, Dr Waugh would not give them proper medical attendance'.

The case was heard at Wells Assizes on 13th July, 1889, and my great-grandfather lost it. Hence the bill. No amount of filial piety can disguise the fact that it is a very funny and a very beautiful thing when people who bring actions for libel or slander lose them. But the final piece in the jigsaw only fell into place last week, at Brighton.

Needless to say, there were few people one wished to meet among the dim, vulgar and avaricious faces which gather together for the Conservative Party Conference, but it was a great pleasure to recognise another Somerset landowner in the throng, Mr William Rees-Mogg, who lives near Midsomer Norton. In London, he is better known as the distinguished and influential editor of a national daily newspaper called *The Times*.

Rees-Mogg, whom I saw at a cocktail party of the Bow Group, was kind enough to say how much he had enjoyed reading about my great-grandfather in the *Evening Standard*. Our two great-grandfathers had been well known to each other, he said. He had often meant to thank me for the kindness my ancestor once showed to his.

By coincidence, the Rees-Mogg had been struck down in

his death agony just outside my great-grandfather's house in Midsomer Norton, and Dr Waugh hastened to give him proper medical attendance. All in vain. Two great-grandsons grew misty eyed at the poignancy of it.

The oddest thing about the bill, from Messrs Rees-Mogg and Davy, which is a handsome object secured by green riband, is that it never seems to have been paid. Why, I wonder, did my great-grandfather decide to preserve the bill but not the receipt, if there ever was a receipt? The obvious explanation is that the bill was never paid, that my great-grandfather murdered his creditor, signing the death certificate himself and swearing that the victim had absolved him from his debts as he died.

I hope mine is not the true explanation. If it is, this poor Rees-Mogg was probably shot and then poisoned by the son of the man who christened him. Dr Alexander Waugh's father was Rev James Hay Waugh, the blameless Rector of Corsley, whom I described earlier. It would be a sad thing if two Somerset land-owning families were to fall out about a murder committed more than eighty years ago, when both were Protestant and before either discovered their enthusiasm for the Common Market and this wonderful man called Roy Jenkins. Besides, now that I have retired to Somerset, I should like to give a little thought to my obituary notice in *The Times*.

What is he trying to do to Somerset?

Combe Florey, Somerset.

No sooner was the Waugh family settled in Somerset than Mr Peter Walker announced his intention of taking away a third of the county's population and a large part of its rateable value. From being fourteenth in size of population, with 597,000 inhabitants, Somerset will become forty-first out of forty-four, with ony 385,000. Perhaps something I wrote somewhere displeased Mr Walker. Or perhaps he was influenced by friendly rivalry with the Conservative Member for Taunton, Mr Edward du Cann, a fellow pioneer in the unit trust business.

I am joking, of course. The idea that anyone as clean-looking as my old friend Peter Walker could be influenced by anything except the highest motives is laughable. We may find it hard to decide exactly what his high motives were on this occasion, but the law still allows us to guess.

The Times has suggested that his decision was governed by

a desire to pack the new county of Avon with Conservative voters. If so, we can applaud the intention while trembling for its success. Feeling among the inhabitants of North Somerset runs very high, and few of them are likely to vote Conservative with great relish in their new environment. One hears the most disgraceful remarks made about Mr Peter Walker personally.

For my own part, I have never much cared for North Somerset, having spent many of the most boring and unpleasant years of my short life at school there. I count few personal friends among the 212,000 Somerset men who are being banished.

Bath is a pleasant enough city, it is true, as well as being the spot where the first King of all England was crowned in 973, but Mr Walker can't be expected to know about that sort of thing and the citizens of Bath forfeited all claim to our sympathy when they put a main sewer pipe through Mr L. P. Hartley's garden, causing that venerable novelist much distress when it blew up a few months later. Plainly, the city has been taken over by hooligans and richly deserves to be a satellite of the Bristol conurbation.

For the rest, Somerset will surely survive without the mudflats of Weston-super-Mare. Bristolians want somewhere to take their ladies of a Sunday afternoon; here they can bask in the mud like so many hippopotami. The last time I visited Weston-super-Mare was on the day of the Coronation, with another boy called Green-Armytage. The town did its best to look festive for the occasion, achieving the standard of jubilation which one might expect at a Jewish funeral in New York.

Midsomer Norton, which is also being added to Bristol, has gone downhill since the days when my great-grandfather ministered to its ailments. His house is now used as local government offices. Perhaps mini-Peter Walkers sit around there, dreaming of the day when they can declare that Torquay is part of Surrey, or Dorking is a suburb of Liverpool.

Nor, for my own part, have I ever been able to see the point of Radstock. The people of North-east Somerset, in my experience, are a surly, embittered race, shifty and brutal by turns – more like Welshmen than Englishmen, more like small monkeys than human beings. One can't help feeling that Mr Walker may be doing something wise and statesmanlike when he encloses them all in a sort of Bantustan with the city-dwellers of Bristol and Bath. One might almost feel sorry for Bristol, suddenly invaded by 315,000 surly, yellow-toothed midgets from Midsomer Norton and Radstock; by the squelching, lugubrious inhabitants of Weston-super-Mare and by whooping sewage-pipe maniacs from Bath.

But then one reflects that Bristol is the city which has returned Mr Wedgwood Benn to Parliament for the last twenty-one years, electing him even when he was manifestly unable to take his seat, being a peer in addition to his other unfortunate handicaps. Bristol richly deserves whatever Mr Walker has in store for it.

The most curious part of the whole amazingly pointless initiative is the administration's latest changes of mind. The town of Frome is to be allowed to stay in Somerset, and so are a few small villages, including Ston Easton. Frome is the home town of Mr Christopher Hollis, the ex-MP and man of letters who has been in the forefront of those writing letters to *The Times* against Mr Walker's scheme. Ston Easton is, of course, the village of Mr Rees-Mogg, *The Times*'s benign and much-loved editor. One also notices how the new boundary just manages to skirt clear of Mr Anthony Powell, the fashion-abe novelist, at Chantry. It begins to look as if after its tussle with Mr L. P. Hartley over his sewer at Bath, the Ministry of Local Government has decided to leave writers and other literary gentlemen alone.

Somerset County Council is resolutely opposed to losing a third of its dominion. Since its chairman is a neighbour and friend, I must watch my step. Moreover, the Council is considering plans to convert the disused Taunton-Minehead railway line at Combe Florey, within sight of my windows, into a 'transit caravan site and picnic area for recreational purposes'. So one doesn't want to annoy the County Council at

59

this stage. The local newspaper, the *Somerset County Gazette*, is also upset about losing the 'northern growth area' of the county. Since I will probably apply for the job of writing its nature notes before I am through, I had better watch my step.

But both these organisations must realise that their own anxieties are not universally shared.

The pride and the joy of living in Somerset have nothing to do with northern growth areas. They are something much more fundamental than that. Perhaps, for Somerset to survive it was necessary for her to shrink a little. What makes her the finest jewel in the crown of England is precisely that she has not yet succumbed to the Peter Walker philosophy of growth, nor to the statist tyrannies of Mr Wedgwood Benn.

When the crown falls to pieces Somerset will still have the coalmines of the Mendips for warmth and electricity, access to the sea and enough acres to feed itself many times over, while the wretched burghers of Bristol and the furtive, rat-like inhabitants of the countryside around die like flies.

The County Council of Somerset would be better employed preparing to crater all roads East, offering a cash reward for the scalps of any planners found polluting her pure, sweet air and commissioning her native writers and musicians to prepare an anthem to celebrate freedom and independence from Messrs Walker and Wedgwood Benn.

The day I played chicken with my dinner

Combe Florey, Somerset.

Mr Barber's request that we should all spend more money to provide employment for each other has certainly not gone unanswered down here.

The refurbishment of my little old family home at present occupies twenty-two men full-time : plumbers, plasterers, electricians, decorators, bricklayers and carpenters, they arrive every morning in limousines which stretch as far as the eye can see, glittering in the cold winter sunlight.

Unlike great builders of the past – Louis XIV, Pope Leo de' Medici, King Solomon – I spend most of my time handing round cups of tea to the workmen, with the result that I now have a warm sympathy for the poor man who tried to build a tower at Babel. One of the only countries still unrepresented in the Combe Florey work-force is Red China. If any Chinese lady would like to come and help with the tea, I should be most grateful. By the time the bills arrive, I expect Mr Barber will have declared another freeze, so I won't even have a medal for conspicuous gallantry in the employment drive to take with me on my travels.

A house decorator who came with us from Wiltshire is the greatest comfort at the present time. He prefers sailing to driving around in a limousine and has two beautiful sailing boats. After an accident in his youth, he became hard of hearing, and derives a certain wry amusement from the way people tend to treat the deaf as if they were mentally defective as well.

In fact, he is one of the true philosophers of our time. One day, the Government presented him with a plastic apparatus to help his hearing, whether out of genuine concern for his health or the usual reckless bossiness. He was so appalled by the noise of the modern world and by the boredom of what people were saying to each other that he threw it away immediately and has resisted all attempts to give him another.

He is a vegetarian, which often seems to bring out the contemplative side in a man. Few of us would eat meat if we really thought about what me were doing. My butcher in Bishop's Lydeard is an obliging man and I have often noticed that his meat is particularly fresh. Last week, my wife wanted to order some calves' livers and the butcher said she'd have to wait while he killed a calf. She assumed he was joking, and was horrified to notice that the liver was steaming when he brought it in. Next, she wanted a leg of lamb. The butcher looked at her oddly: 'We are being difficult this morning, aren't we? You will have to wait ten minutes for that,' he said. My wife decided she could do without, and now we are living on a diet of eggs.

Eggs, too, have their worrying side, even if nobody has yet claimed that they have immortal souls. When we lived in Wiltshire we used to buy our chickens from a neighbouring farmer. One day he was ill, but his wife said we could take a chicken if I killed it myself.

I am much bigger than the average English chicken, and furthermore I was armed with a rolling pin and a kitchen knife. As a matter of fact, I have always had the greatest contempt for chickens. They are so stupid that they probably don't even notice the difference when they die, but I must admit that this particular chicken put up a very good fight.

For the first time, I began to understand how the Ancient Mariner felt about his Albatross as I carried the bleeding corpse down the village street to my house, and I have never enjoyed eating a chicken less :

> An orphan's curse would drag to hell
> A spirit from on high
> But oh ! more horrible than that
> Is the curse in a chicken's eye.

Animals and religion are the two subjects to avoid in newspaper articles, as I know to my cost. It must be particularly dangerous to discuss religion so soon after Mr Wilson's visit to Ulster, when the whole nation held its breath in case the plucky little fellow came to any harm. However, it would be absurd to deny that while in Berkshire I attended a Roman Catholic christening in a Church of England village church. That morning I had taken the children to the nearest Catholic church, a leaky old hut packed with worshippers and decorated with pictures of racehorses. My dear wife, however, who is of the Anglican persuasion, attended the Church of England shrine, which was handsome but contained only nine other worshippers.

For the christening in the afternoon the Anglican and Catholic clergymen both got kitted up (no redundancy created), the church was packed, and a good time was had by all in pleasant surroundings.

This seems the obvious solution to the problem of both churches. The C. of E. has plenty of money – over £340 million of interest-yielding assets – and some magnificent churches but very few worshippers to benefit. Roman Catholics in England have plenty of worshippers but no money and their churches are for the most part rather makeshift, not to say scruffy. It is high time the so-called ecumenical dialogue was taken away from the theologians and put in the capable hands of someone like Sir Charles Clore or Mr Jim Slater.

This presupposes that there is no essential difference in the consumer product, and I honestly think that only a pedant or a professional theologian can tell which twin has the Toni nowadays. The one logical reason for people to stay away from Anglican churches must be that they are frightened off by the clergymen's wives, since Catholic priests are still not allowed to marry. I think that Convocation of Canterbury should consider this matter.

Perhaps wives are also to blame for the extraordinary sheepishness of Anglican clergymen in the present time. When the great Sydney Smith was Rector of Combe Florey in the 1830s he used to tie antlers on his donkey's head in the Rectory garden, in order to mock a neighbouring landowner who was turning his fields into a deer park. There is no longer any Rector of Combe Florey, but I can see very few of Mr Smith's successors daring to tie so much as an Easter bonnet on a budgerigar. It all comes back to Women's Lib. Personally, I think that many clergymen would be a great deal better off without their wives, and I am delighted to see that the Pope, for once, seems to agree with me.

All this talk of religion and animals can only produce a host of letters pointing out the obvious errors in everything I have said. The last time I said anything controversial it was about the horoscopes of P. G. Wodehouse and Picasso. An astrologer called Mr Derek Parker very kindly sent me a copy of his latest book, *The Compleat Astrologer* (Mitchell Beazley, £5.95), a massive tome which reveals how to cast horoscopes. It is much more difficult than one might suppose.

However, if anyone wishes to give me the benefit of his advice on religion or animals or both, I should be most grateful if he could also supply the exact date, time, place of his birth so that I can judge the influence of the planets on each complaint.

Go and play your beastly game somewhere else

Combe Florey, Somerset.

There are some crimes against nature so gross and so unspeakable that one can only gasp and rub one's eyes. Few people will suspect that such a crime is imminent when I say that an application has been made to build an eighteen-hole championship golf course in the Quantocks. There are much uglier things than golf courses, after all – it might have been a power station, or a giant sewage processing plant. One has little sympathy for women who complain that they have been raped, when they might so easily have been murdered as well.

There are only twenty-seven places in England scheduled as Areas of Outstanding Natural Beauty. The Quantock Forest and Hills are one of them. They are not the same thing as the National Parks, which are intended as popular recreation areas and which have to be equipped with car parks, public lavatories, snack bars and all the other amenities which the British public likes to find in the countryside. Areas of Outstanding Natural Beauty are set aside for the much smaller number of really serious nature fanatics, ramblers, poets and so on – those who are prepared to put up with a little discomfort to contemplate the beauties of nature.

The Quantocks have all this and powerful literary associations too : Wordsworth lived at Alfoxden and Coleridge at Nether Stowey to write their Lyrical Ballads together. It could be said that the Quantocks were the cradle for the entire school of nineteenth- and twentieth-century English nature poetry.

The proposed golf course above Crowcombe will practically

cut this unique and tiny area into two parts with its club house and bar, its access roads and car parks. Somerset is so used to its beauty that the authorities take it for granted. Both the Rural District Council and the County Council have accepted this wicked proposal.

There is already a perfectly good golf course at Bridgwater a few miles away, even if it is less exclusive and less expensive than the new one. Never mind that this appalling scheme will bring an undesirable class of person into the neighbourhood – loud-voiced businessmen from the Midlands who will discriminate against each other in various unpleasant and inexplicable ways, violating our womenfolk and making the night hideous with their brutal laughter. Never mind that there are only thirty-eight square miles of the Quantocks while there are 53,884 square miles of England and Wales which are outside the Quantocks and not scheduled as Areas of Outstanding Natural Beauty for these wretched people to play their championship golf. This golf course may well be a crime against nature, but the most important thing is that it is directly contrary to Government policy for Areas of Outstanding Natural Beauty; amenities and suchlike filth may be supplied in the National Parks, but not in AONBs.

Let us hope that when the heroic Mr Peter Walker gets to hear of Somerset County Council's behaviour, the towns of Sodom and Gomorrah will reckon they got off lightly.

In the unlikely event of Mr Walker's neglecting to do his duty, I shall reveal some of the plans of the Action Committee for saving the Quantocks, which meets secretly at the Sign of the Quantock Weaver in Over Stowey over cups of tea supplied by the Misses Dickinson and Biddulph. We march under the banner of Mrs Jane Tarr, headmistress of Kingston St Mary School, and Mr Walker will pray to be delivered to the Angry Brigade before we have finished with him.

We are a law-abiding community for the most part in Somerset, and I always think this is probably because of the affection and respect we feel towards our police force. However, last week an Upminster magistrate, Dr Ernest Anthony, made the most amazing allegations of corruption against the Somerset police in an article he wrote for the legal journal *Justice of the Peace.*

Obviously, I cannot speak for the Essex police, over whom Dr Anthony is a magistrate, but I have always believed that the Somerset force was one of the least corrupt in the country.

The reason for Dr Anthony's charge is apparently that on a visit to Somerset his car was held up by followers of the Devon and Somerset Stag Hounds, some of whom, he claimed, were driving without due care and attention. Furthermore, he could see no policemen around. This leads him to assert that the entire Somerset police force is 'in the pockets of the Devon and Somerset Hunt'. I could point out to Dr Anthony, if I wished, that the Somerset roads are really made for stag hunting, not travelling from A to B.

On Sundays, when the whole of Somerset takes its Granny out for a drive, nobody can travel at more than ten miles an hour in any direction, since there is never any question of being able to pass. We are proud of our roads. But the matter has gone beyond friendly recrimination. Dr Anthony has accused our police of corruption.

This is an extremely serious matter. When magistrates of one county join the 'Knock-the-Police' campaign in another, I think the time has come for an investigation.

A land fit for businessmen to fly over and drive off

Combe Florey, Somerset.
Christmas is a time when even the smartest town mice begin to think of their country cousins.

Any countryman who goes up to London at this time to buy himself a new leather smock in Carnaby Street for Christmas or whatever returns a sadder and a wiser man. Perhaps townsfolk still feel a little thrill when they realise that there is an alternative society waiting for them if ever they should decide to drop out.

We country folk stand by our gates trying to look quaint and Christmassy, waiting for the great rush to arrive at our end. Perhaps a few townspeople would like to pause between mouthfuls of rich food this weekend and reflect on how nice it is to have a bit of country left to come and eat it in. Our function is to make townspeople happy in other ways, too. By comparing their lives to our own, with its appalling discomforts and inconveniences, the narrowness of its intellectual, cultural and social horizons they can entertain the illusion of having chosen to live in the towns because they prefer it. And a few of them like to see the occasional wild flower, too, when summer comes round.

So the countryside has a point. It is not just another good cause, like the dear old Church of England. The reason I mention the Quantocks at Christmas time is nothing to do with the religious festival, but merely because many fellow citizens happen to be thinking of the countryside.

The Quantocks are not to be confused with old-age pensioners, who may be feeling the cold at this time of year, or with Bangladesh. They are a group of hills, measuring scarcely more than six miles by six miles, which happen to exist in Somerset, fringed by gorse and bracken, inhabited mostly by wild deer, wild ponies and the occasional badger.

Another inhabitant is called Mr Nick Bucknall, a farmer of great charm and frankness. He could sell his 250-acre farm on the Quantocks for £60,000, he says, not because this is its agricultural value – the land is very poor and the house isolated – but because of its position, described as one of the most beautiful sites in England. Instead, however, he has been approached by a consortium who plan to turn the area into a £400,000 golf course.

If this is allowed to happen, England will have lost an area of outstanding natural beauty, through which every Englishman has the right to roam. It will also, of course, have gained a first-class golf course, where a handful of over-fed businessmen can work off their surplus fat. This useful function might even help the export drive in some obscure way and make us all a little richer.

Mr Bucknall suggests that a golf course will be prettier to look at than his silly old fields. Somerset County Council agrees to the extent that it is even hiring a barrister, out of ratepayers' money, to support Mr Bucknall's interests at the public inquiry ordered by Mr Peter Walker.

Perhaps at Christmas, people will be able to recognise the unspeakable iniquity of this. The tiny enclave of the Quantocks can contain an area of outstanding natural beauty, or it can contain a golf course. It cannot contain both. The country elected this present Government and Somerset elected its County Council in the pathetic belief that they would try to conserve what was beautiful and worthwhile. Instead, we are building a country fit only for the businessmen to fly over between desultory waddles along a fairway from green to green.

Can Mr Heath's Government really have sunk to that? His greatest monument in a hundred years' time, when the last noxious gases of the revolting Concorde aeroplane have been dissipated, when the last supersonic bang has sounded, will be that he wiped the Quantocks off the map of England and put a golf course there instead.

What can the concerned citizen do? Apparently he can appoint himself into an Action Committee and squabble a little about a sub-committee. He can ask his fellow citizens to sign a petition if he has the time. At a first meeting of the Save the Quantocks Action Committee, in Kingston St. Mary Village school, I was a little alarmed to find myself announced as chairman of a sub-committee for handling the media. There are no other members of this sub-committee, I understand, unless I can convene some.

Well, if anybody would like to be convened or handled, here I am. There are no rich people in this neighbourhood to answer the voice of money in its own currency. We do not even have any newspaper proprietors here, unlike the residents of Wing, in Buckinghamshire, so it looks as if the Quantocks will softly and silently fade away.

Just watch out, in the weeks after Christmas, for a plump, balding man pacing the streets of London in a leather smock from Carnaby Street, with what is obviously an atom bomb in his arms and a purposeful look in his terrible, staring eyes.

Wanted: A thin lad to sweep my chimneys ...

Combe Florey, Somerset.
A neighbour I saw out shooting on Monday told me he had seen an old man with two heads being pushed in a pram on the Gloucestershire-Warwickshire border some years ago. Two members of the party remembered a local figure who had fox pads instead of feet. The story was that his mother had gone out hunting too soon before her confinement, although there were other, more sinister explanations.

Some time ago, a farmer swore to me that he had seen a ghost climbing the ruined church tower in a village called Upton between here and Dulverton, so he sat at the bottom of the tower all night waiting for it to come down again. . . .

Conversation somehow acquires a new dimension in the countryside, where people meet and talk less than they do in the towns. I sometimes wonder how the stories we tell each other would go down in fashionable London. Would lovely Lady Dartmouth be alarmed? Would the gifted John Wells add them to his repertory? Would Mr Kenneth Tynan try to perform them in the nude?

My elder son, Alexander, and my youngest brother, Septimus, sometimes complain about ghosts they meet on the stairs, but ghosts are among the smaller problems of living in a huge mansion in the country. Disasters of Old Testament magnitude may strike without warning at any moment – a ceiling will collapse, water will run up the walls in defiance of every natural law, a little mushroom peeping between the floorboards will herald a new outbreak of dry rot.

Mansions may be rather cheaper to buy than bungalows, on

average nowadays, but in order to enjoy living in one you must see these problems in the perspective of eternity, cultivating the fecklessness of a Tibetan hermit. The only alternative is to be rich, but the rich nowadays live in a different kind of purgatory, tortured by the fear of losing their servants. A neighbour in Wiltshire needed a whole month's notice before he could ask anyone to tea, so that he could prepare his servants for the shock of having to lay an extra cup and saucer.

Even the most ambitious or insanely optimistic man nowadays would do well to reconcile himself to a future without the comforts of a butler and footmen.

When we decided to convert the huge old dining room into a kitchen-diner we thought we were making a profound statement about modern society and the future role of the middle classes inside it. Similarly when we converted the old kitchen into a nursery, playroom, junior citizen's recreation area or whatever.

But how does the enlightened modern man cope with old-fashioned chimneys which need cleaning? Rumour has it you fire a shotgun up them, but this does not seem to me an entirely sane way to behave on the strength of a rumour. There are irons for a boy to climb up, but people say it is illegal to send boys up chimneys ever since poor mad William Blake wrote such disturbing poems on the subject :

A little black thing among the snow,
Crying weep, weep in tones of woe !
Where are thy father and mother? Say?
They are both gone up to the church to pray.

My own sons would be only too delighted to climb the chimney, but I doubt whether they would leave it any cleaner. Older boys in the neighbourhood, even those from the poorest homes, are much too fat nowadays and would almost certainly get stuck. In fact, I have often noticed that it is the poorest homes which produce the fattest children. Knowledgeable and concerned friends assure one that this is because their diet is unbalanced – too much potato, not enough

meat – but personal observation leads me to suppose that it is because they eat too many sweets. For some no doubt very complicated reason, poorer parents are usually more indulgent to their children than richer ones. It may be that sweets have a harmful effect on intellectual development, which would clear up much boring controversy about heredity and environment.

Be that as it may, the fact remains that for as long as parents continue to stuff their children with sweets, nobody is going to be able to clean my chimneys. A swingeing tax on sweets might be the answer – far more sensible than Prince Philip's Baby Tax – except that bitter experience leads one to suppose that parents would absorb the charge in an increased wage claim and only sweet-loving old age pensioners would suffer. With all our technology, there is no machine to sweep an old-fashioned chimney.

However, there is one modern invention of which you can take the fullest advantage in a huge mansion – this wonderful new thing called the Generation Gap. My children's quarters are about forty paces from the room where I write, and everybody is happier for it. Apart from the convenience of this arrangement, it seems to me that the best monument one can leave nowadays is a clutch of children who are not spoiled, over-supervised psychopaths. The time is surely past for

74

building more lasting memorials than that, and we should concentrate on self-effacement.

In Ireland, they still put crosses on the side of the road where somebody has been killed in a driving accident but even these monuments have lost much of their poignancy through their being too many of them. Motoring near Barnstaple, in North Devon, I was sad to see the new monument to Caroline Thorpe on Codden Hill. Of course, one understands Mr Jeremy Thorpe's wish to create some permanent public memorial to his private grief, and the Portland stone column is not nearly as obtrusive as it might have been, even if it lacks the grandeur of the Wellington memorial in neighbouring Somerset, or the delightful intimacy of the St John monuments at Lydiard Tregoze, in Wiltshire.

Nevertheless, I would be happy to think that now he has built it and had the Archbishop of Canterbury down to bless it he will decide that a much better public memorial to his wife would be if he restored a little corner of Exmoor on Codden Hill to its natural beauty.

If he can decide that, and if he quietly take the monument down again, he will have left a memorial to himself and to his wife for which we can all be grateful. He will also have earned greater respect from posterity than Mr Heath has yet earned, despite his £36,000 prize for statesmanship, and greater respect than Mr Wilson has yet earned with all his miserable £200,000-worth of memoirs.

Can a mole dig a ton of coal?

Combe Florey, Somerset.

Coal-miners on strike can be sure of warm sympathy from anyone who has ever commuted on British Rail's Western Region. The 7.50 from Taunton to Paddington is probably rather dirtier than most coal mines, but there is the same comradeship which can only come from shared suffering and the same cheerful defeatism which old people remember from wartime and call the Singapore Spirit.

Instead of whistling 'Colonel Bogy' and making jokes in rhyming slang with Cockney accents to keep our spirits up, we veterans of the 7.50 tend to fall asleep over our copies of *The Times*. Our mouths hang open and most of us snore, as the dirt settles slowly on our faces. At Paddington we wake up from a hundred unattractive postures and shamble down the platform like itinerant Negro minstrels, pink tongues licking at our blackened lips.

Do coal-miners ever fall asleep underground, I wonder?

Probably not often. In the 7.50 from Taunton, I often watch my fellow passengers snoring away with their bowler hats in place of the miner's pit helmet on the rack above them, and wonder which member of the Royal family they are dreaming about. Sometimes it seems likely that they are having a gentle, voluptuous dream about Princess Margaret in an eastern setting; at other times they are obviously having a ghastly nightmare about Princess Anne.

Last week, *The Times* printed a large photograph of Princess Anne as a commandant of the St John Ambulance Brigade. I am not one of those people given to lodging complaints with the Press Council, but if the Editor of *The Times* had seen the havoc he caused in the 7.50 from Taunton, I am sure he would choose his photographs more carefully in future. The shrieks and strangled groans from dreamers in other compartments were bad enough; more pitiful by far was the state of the man sitting opposite me, who had fallen asleep with his newspaper open at the photograph of the radiant young Princess.

I have seen sights in my time to chill the blood of the hardiest, but I have never seen a look of such mortal terror on any human face before. Between Westbury and Pewsey his hair had turned grey; by the time the train pulled out of Reading Central, it was snow-white.

Not snow-white for long, of course, on the Western Region.

*   *   *

The extreme dirt of our cities makes motoring equally confusing nowadays. Last weekend I tried to motor from Somerset to stay with some friends in Nottinghamshire but got stuck for several hours in Birmingham where no motorway will go and where the city fathers refuse to put up signposts pointing farther than the suburbs. Who on earth knows whether Perry Bar is on the way to Nottingham, or Bristol, or Blackpool? The classic solution in this sort of predicament is to ask a native the way, if you think you can understand his answer. But native Brummies are impossible to distinguish nowadays, and every time I approached someone,

77

he smiled inscrutably : Of course, he would be delighted to explain the quickest route from Chittagong to Rawalpindi, or even to Samarkand, but Nottingham was quite impossible. It might be anywhere.

The only way to distinguish autochthonous from immigrant Brummies nowadays is by their teeth : immigrants' teeth tend to be whiter. But it makes driving rather hazardous if you must always be carrying out a dental inspection of passers-by, and it would surely be easier if the Birmingham city fathers could put up a few ordinary signposts.

So before we allow ourselves to be swept off our feet by a tidal wave of sympathy for the miners, we might reflect on a few of the sorrows they are spared : they don't have to live in Birmingham or review modern novels; suffer the vituperation of literary gentlemen or the impertinence of secretaries; receive writs by every post alleging libel, and so on. We might also reflect a little on the habits of the mole, which spends most of its life digging underground without expecting or receiving the smallest amount of sympathy from anyone.

Nothing is less funny than those stale, sneering remarks about the British working man which elderly people used to make when they thought nobody else was listening. I am one of those who happen to believe that the typical British worker works extremely hard.

But it is a curious fact about moles, according to Dr Kenneth Mellanby's beautiful book on the subject [*The Mole,* Collins, £2] that the typical British mole works about twelve times harder. Although he only shifts 30 lb. of soil in an hour, this is apparently the equivalent of a twelve stone miner moving twelve tons an hour; whereas British miners do not move more than twenty-three cwt. an hour from the coal-face.

There are those who will say that this is not a fair comparison, since the mole naturally digs underground for worms, grubs and other food. Coal does not have quite the same appeal even from the most patriotic coalminer, although, of course, babies and dogs eat it with relish. In fact, this argument does not stand up. Moles could live above ground per-

fectly well, if they chose to do so, eating slugs and cater-
pillars in season.

The reason they choose to live underground digging tunnels
in every direction – surely the most lonely and fatuous way of
covering the distance between two points ever devised – is
because they can't bear each other's company. Or so Dr
Mellanby leads one to believe. Although they live happily
together as small children for about a month, being breast-
fed by their mother in a nest of dry grass and leaves, they
become solitary in later life and fight to the death if they meet.
They never breed in captivity. In the circumstances, their
courtship and mating patterns remain a mystery, as do those
of so many people. It may be that the mole's industrious
habits explain the term 'blackleg'. This has often puzzled
me when used in the labour movement to describe someone
who, whether through inadvertence or temporary insanity, has
done a good day's work. I don't know.

All I do know is that if Mr Heath could breed moles by
the hundred thousand and train them to dig for coal in the
same way that dogs and pigs are trained to dig for truffles,
then all his troubles would be over. Or at any rate some of
them would be.

Bypass Bridgwater — You know it makes scents . . .

Combe Florey, Somerset.

The town of Bridgwater, eleven miles to the north of here, has a most unpleasant smell. Its position, straddling the A38 Birmingham to Exeter main road, makes it the gateway to the South West, and its peculiar smell serves the entire West Country in the office of a wall or as a moat defensive to a house against the envy of less happier lands. Holidaymakers from the West Midlands have been known to turn back in

disgust and take the next plane to sunny Majorca, while its effect on honeymoon couples has been even more serious. Many a wedding night has come to grief in a tumult of accusation and counter-accusation when the nuptial car, bound for the gentle cabbage smells of Torquay and Ilfracombe has entered the appalling stench of Bridgwater.

The smell has been there for forty years, ever since British

Cellophane Ltd. opened a factory in the hungry Thirties. Nobody in Bridgwater minds it in the least, explaining in a sentimental voice that it helps to create jobs. A spokesman for British Cellophane said : 'It's a bit overdone this talk about smells . . . it's the sort of smell you get in thousands of back streets in Birmingham; only because Bridgwater is in the middle of the country people complain.'

Suddenly however, last week, the Town Council decided to act. One wonders what pressure was brought to bear, since activity of any sort is quite rightly discouraged in Somerset. Even in its frenzied activism of last week, the Bridgwater Town Council did not go as far as doing anything to remove the smell. Instead, it started asking for reports and issuing statements : the Health Committee asked the Medical Officer (Dr R. H. Watson) to comment on the odour, and Dr Watson solemnly affirmed that no deleterious side-effects were apparent on any of the babies and children of Bridgwater who visited his clinic.

Life expectancy in Bridgwater was no shorter than in the rest of Somerset, testified Dr Watson. He asked the County Analyst, Miss Joan Peden, for support, and she, in turn, invited the Chief Alkali Inspector to give his opinion. All were convinced that the smell's active chemical ingredients were within permissible levels of safety.

Nobody suggested that it was good for you, assisting vigorous hair growth and improving sexual proficiency, but the burden of their song was that the people of Bridgwater were jolly lucky to have such a benign smell among them and should thank their lucky stars for it.

A connoisseur of modern smells assures me that after Bridgwater he might easily mistake the Slough sewage farm (well known to travellers on the M4) for Waterers' Floral Mile. The inhabitants of Bridgwater, of course, no longer notice it, but they are prepared to accept its presence in order to preserve their own grossly inflated wage levels. These are already a scandal throughout the farming community, making a mockery of truth, justice and lasting values. Any of us, we feel, could earn as much if we were prepared to make a disgusting smell about it. We prefer to be poor and fragrant.

The degradation of Bridgwater's inhabitants, it seems to me, illustrates something which is happening to large sections of the community nowadays. Our politicians continue to live in dread of a national conscience which will one day arise and smite them – when they have shot one demonstrator too many in Ulster, or tortured one suspect a little too vigorously – but the national conscience no longer exists, except among a handful of troublemakers.

People are still prepared to look sentimental about their own prosperity, and students are prepared to demonstrate about their own rights and privileges, but nobody cares about anyone else.

The reason why the Town Council of Bridgwater has suddenly decided to take an interest in the town's smell after forty years is probably something to do with the M5 motorway which has been crawling its way down from Bristol without making any impression on the national consciousness. When completed, this will open the beauties of the West Country to the flat accents and the jingling pockets of the industrial Midlands. No wonder Bridgwater is suddenly anxious to convince the world that there are no health hazards involved in the town's appalling smell.

Motorways are themselves a sign of the moral degradation of our times. The Suez Canal, people used to say, was built on the bones of tens of thousands of Egyptian labourers who died building it. Travellers on luxury cruises through the Suez Canal (in the days when the Suez Canal was open), often used to spare a tear for all the poor Gyppoes. Nobody nowadays pauses to think how much misery and heartbreak has gone into every yard of a new motorway – how many homes have been demolished or made uninhabitable, how many farmers dispossessed.

The Health Committee of Bridgwater Town Council were quite wrong to say that the town's smell has done no injury to health. It may not have caused the citizens' hair to fall, or impaired their sexual proficiency, but it has impaired their moral perceptions and brought them a step nearer to the level of animals or robots.

The new motorway will take holidaymakers dangerously near the town. . . .

Nine months to Gormley's Bulge . . .

Combe Florey, Somerset.

During the war, a neighbouring landowner in Devon was reported to the authorities for spreading alarm and despondency, which was an offence then. He had probably been complaining about the shortage of pheasants on the western front until he was overheard by the Thought Police.

Nobody down here knows what powers Mr Maudling has assumed with his emergency proclamation but if they include imprisonment for spreading alarm and despondency he had better declare the whole West Country a prison camp and go back to sleep.

My own pathetic attempts to bring sunshine and comfort have nearly led to a lynching. I tried it on a farmer who had been up since four o'clock in the morning to finish milking before the first power cut. The evening before he had helped milk nearly a hundred cows by hand in the dark. Whenever cows are upset by a change in their routine, they show it by lifting their tails and making a mess. Either his cows were extremely upset, or they were demonstrating solidarity with the miners, but he was not looking forward to his next dung bath. Perhaps it was tactless of me to urge him to think of his lucky chickens in their deep-litter houses able to get a little sleep at last as a result of the strike.

In fact, the miners' strike could prove very good news for farmers, if only they would listen to me instead of rushing round in circles and spreading alarm and despondency. Until now they have had no effective way of protesting against inadequate subsidies or guaranteed prices except to stage pathetic, student-style demonstrations, driving tractors through the nearest country town and suchlike tomfoolery.

Farmers can't bring the nation to its knees by refusing to sell their meat or dairy produce, because if they do the nation will just go and buy it much cheaper from New Zealand or Scandinavia. They would be left with a lot of rotting food and, for the duration of the strike, they would lose all the complicated subsidies which become payable whenever a farmer sneezes, cleans his teeth or puts on a new shirt, provided he remembers to apply to the Ministry on each occasion.

But now the miners have shown the way. All the farmers have to do is to picket the power stations. Within days, the nation will start worrying about its old age pensioners, cruelly deprived of their delicious electricity after a lifetime of service to the community. All the paper pounds Mr Heath can print will be poured into the farmers' laps.

So much for the Dunkirk spirit. In fact, West Countrymen never seemed to share the general enthusiasm for World War II, resenting America's occupation of Devon and Somerset much more than they seemed to resent Hitler's occupation of the Polish Corridor. In the present emergency they make it plain that they are prepared to put up with considerable privations in order to deprive miners of their just wages, but only so long as they can be sure that the miners are not going to win at the end of the day.

It is that thought which really causes alarm and despondency.

This is an aspect of political psychology which the politicians seem to have overlooked. I am sure that many countrymen would be quite happy to do without shoes and socks if one told them that by doing so they were depriving some crane drivers in Newcastle of a wage increase. It is only in the towns, where people seem to regard electricity as an inalienable birthright, that a real scream of pain goes up every time they lose an amp or an erg.

One would have thought that with so much to see in modern urban society which is ugly, town folk would be content to sit in the dark for a while.

Nine months after the great power strike in New York everybody was interested to note a significant rise in the birthrate. Many explanations were offered : that New Yorkers who are repelled by their own hideousness when they can see each other overcome this difficulty in the dark; or that New York women are so wired and plugged with electrical family planning devices that men often mistake them for a bedside lamp and can only make head or tail of them during a power strike.

My own explanation is much simpler. It cannot be an accident that Benjamin Franklin, who invented electricity, was also the first man to raise the world population scare. Electricity was invented to stop people having babies. Franklin knew perfectly well that people who were going to spend all evening watching a load of rubbish on television or playing gramophone records at each other would never get round to propagating their species.

In any case, and whatever the reason, we are plainly going to see a dramatic rise in the birth-rate some nine months hence. Demographers will probably label it the Gormley Bulge, after patient and statesmanlike Joe Gormley, the miners' leader. But we must not suppose it will end there. As people learn how easy it is I can see a whole series of bulges ahead – a Clive Jenkins Bulge, a Jack Jones Bulge, until any Tom, Dick or Harry who can close down the power stations will expect to have a bulge named after him.

Who needs shotguns?

Combe Florey, Somerset.
Taunton, the county town of Somerset, has not seen many of these waves of violence which apparently threaten our British way of life everywhere else. Many people down here who were feeling too lazy to switch off the Prime Minister on Sunday are now rather puzzled.

He seemed to be talking about another country, peopled by unpleasant and avaricious bores who are always hitting each other over the head and then making pompous speeches about it. Even when Mr Wilson put the alternative point of view on Monday, nobody was any the wiser: 'Lawbreaking of all kinds must be ruthlessly pursued and dealt with,' he said. But where do we find all these lawbreakers in Taunton? Applejack brandy has now completely disappeared as a cottage industry, I am sorry to say. A few villains may be driving around Somerset with car licences which are out of date, but most of us feel that we have better things to do with our time than spend it ruthlessly pursuing and dealing with these people.

About fifteen years ago, when television was a new invention. I remember laughing at a Giles cartoon in the *Daily Express* which showed an uncouth farmer standing in a television showroom while one assistant said to the other: 'He wants to know if we have any sets which work on paraffin.'

Many people must have thought along these lines during the electricity cuts, but if television is going to show this sort of rubbish I can't think that many farmers round here would want to waste good paraffin. Nor were these two broad-

casts the sort of thing many of us would wish our children to see.

The children, of course, have been delighted by the coal strike. My unsuccessful attempts to light a primus stove earned the sort of rapturous applause I remember one night in the war when we were allowed on the roof of my Grandmother's house as a treat to watch the bombing of Exeter. In the Great Divide of British politics, which Mr Wilson was boring on about, my children are enthusiastically on the side of the miners, even when I warn them that Mr Heath will probably find it necessary to shoot little children like them before very long.

But there is not much sign of the Great Divide anywhere else. In Taunton, for instance, I find an almost painful degree of unanimity: everybody is united in dislike of Mr Wilson and Mr Heath, of the Tory and Labour parties and everything they stand for, wishing a plague on both their houses and on that of Mr Jeremy Thorpe for good measure.

Mr Heath is planning to make one of his rare visits to Somerset this weekend to address Tory local government officers in the Winter Gardens at Weston-super-Mare. The six Somerset constituencies return six Tory members to Parliament. Continuity, moderation and self-effacement are the only qualities which Somerset expects of its MPs.

Imagine everybody's dismay to discover that the Tory party is now led by a self-styled revolutionary who, for some bizarre reason of his own wants to alter the thousand-year-old boundaries of Somerset itself. Included among the hideous and inexplicable crimes which he proposes against the integrity of Somerset is the forcible removal of Weston-super-Mare, against the wishes of nearly all the inhabitants. I am told that local farmers plan to surround the Winter Gardens with fifty tractors when Mr Heath is inside.

Ostensibly this is no more than a student-style demonstration to support Somerset's integrity, but I think it also springs from a deep-rooted fear that if people like Mr Heath are allowed out of the conference hall to wander the lanes and hills they will pollute the pure, sweet life of Somerset, causing recreational golf courses and businessmen's efficiency colleges to spring up wherever their feet have trodden.

The West Country will not have seen such political activity since the odious, effeminate Duke of Monmouth landed at Lyme Regis (where the sewer is going) and was proclaimed King at Taunton in 1685. After a brief visit from the conscientious Judge Jeffreys, Taunton has been a model of tranquillity ever since. Looking around the town, even on market day when there is far too much traffic for my own rather austere tastes, I can't see that there has been any serious breakdown of law and order. Of course, Somerset may wear quite another aspect after Mr Heath's visit this weekend, and I can't help feeling he would be well advised to stay away.

So far, there has been no need for Somerset men to take their shotguns down from the wall, no departure from 'our traditional British way of doing things' – in Somerset, at least, whatever may be happening in Westminster.

Mr Heath — Victim of the clotted cream?

Combe Florey, Somerset.

The Prime Minister's visit to Somerset has come and gone,
leaving general uneasiness and foreboding behind it. Farmers
have noticed a strange restlessness among their sheep; cattle
have reacted as they always do under these circumstances,
giving birth to seven-headed calves and suchlike. I warned
Mr Heath to stay away from Somerset, but he must have
decided he knew better.

The family's first shock was to see a photograph of Mr
Heath smirking out of the pages of the *Somerset County
Gazette*. He looked oddly and rather endearingly like a
penguin, surrounded by his six Somerset MPs, all laughing
madly while a faint smile played around the lips of their
leader. Perhaps he had been eating the delicious preparation
of malt bread, clotted cream and strawberry jam on which so
many visitors to Somerset come to grief. Perhaps he was just
thinking how he had never imagined, when he was a boy at

Broadstairs, that he would one day get his photograph into the *Somerset County Gazette*.

Worse shocks were in store for us when he opened our copies of the *West Somerset Free Press*. This must be one of the most remarkable newspapers in the country, printed in Williton with a circulation of nearly 11,000 copies. It reports every sporting event in the neighbourhood — where the foxes and stags are found, where they run and how the hunts follow — and seldom announces anything more distressing than the death of an elderly Minehead resident. It devoted an entire page of very small type — about 6,000 words — to describing my grandmother's funeral in Dulverton a few years ago. Here at last one felt, was a newspaper with a true sense of news values. There is nothing lewd or salacious to be found in its pages, nothing unworthy of the beautiful corner of England which fosters it.

Mr Heath never quite dared venture into West Somerset, so there was no reason why the *West Somerset Free Press* should send its faithful reporter on his bicycle all the way to Weston-super-Mare, where the Prime Minister was appearing. Moreover the newspaper is committed to avoiding sensationalism and unpleasantness of every sort. But for some inexplicable reason the Conservatives of Watchet had decided to present Mr Heath with a sextant, and the *West Somerset Free Press* felt bound to record the moment. We shall probably never know why Watchet Conservatives should suddenly take it into their heads to do a silly thing like that. Conceivably it was a form of mass hysteria brought on by pollution in the Bristol Channel from Avonmouth. In any case, Mr Heath seemed to find the presentation as amusing as everyone else, and was laughing like a horse as he accepted the sextant from Mrs Mary Oliver (hon. secretary).

No doubt this sort of thing is all in the day's work for a Prime Minister. When he gets back to Downing Street he will take off his socks, put his new sextant in the cupboard under the stairs and forget the whole dismal episode. But we in West Somerset have longer memories, and it will be a long time before we can get over the shock and horror of finding a stranger in our *Free Press*.

While in Somerset, he received deputations from Somerset County Council to preserve the integrity of Somerset. I have already written about the scheme to redraw the county's thousand-year-old boundaries, enclosing much of the less favoured northern part into a sort of devastation zone around Bath and Bristol under the new name of Avon. Somerset County Council is bitterly opposed to the scheme and spent long hours with Mr Walker and Mr Heath arguing its case.

Most people will be amazed that such a case should need arguing. Anything which has stood for 1,000 years must at least have earned the right not to be destroyed without good reason; and Whitehall has advanced no reason whatever. In fact the whole scheme begins to look like another example of psychotic government, or government for government's sake. Citizens should be on their guard against this tendency, whereby our rulers order people around and change things for no other purpose than the joy of making decisions.

They would be surprised to learn how much political motivation is psychotic in origin. People enter politics or the civil service out of a desire to exert power and influence events; this, I maintain, is an illness. It is only when one realises that great administrators and leaders of men have all been at any rate slightly mad that one has a true understanding of history.

If we subject the present dispute between Somerset County Council and the Government to this rigorous historical analysis we see that the county council's main reason for objecting is that it does not wish to lose power and influence over Weston-super-Mare, Midsomer Norton, Radstock and outlying areas. The question must inevitably arise : what sort of Somerset does the council wish to preserve within its power?

Some weeks ago I reported the council's almost unbelievable acceptance of a proposal to convert a central slab of the Quantock Hills – Britain's first and possibly loveliest area of outstanding natural beauty – into a championship golf course, with club houses, bars and access roads. Every day of the week now the council is buzzing with new schemes for caravan sites and camping areas to exploit the remaining beauty of the area under its control to best advantage.

Last week I discovered that this wretched body has earmarked the sum of exactly £6,000 towards restoring and preserving all the private buildings schedules as being of architectural or historical interest within its boundaries. Other grants are available from the Department of the Environment in London, but these are generally awarded only to buildings of national importance. So far as the county's main character is concerned, this is valued at less than a twentieth part of one per cent of its revenue from rates. The county council would obviously be delighted to preside over a single, vast Butlins holiday camp. I hope Mr Heath will think twice before surrendering completely to the blandishments of clotted cream and strawberry jam.

How my speech saved the village

Combe Florey, Somerset.
Hampstead should send a study group to Somerset village annual meetings before there is more of this heady talk about direct democracy and referenda. Here the people really have their say; resolutions are proposed and votes taken in a text-book model of participation, popular control and the way the tides of history are moving. Sometimes these meetings degenerate, it is true : there was acrimony in the village hall of Combe Florey last year, I gather, when the chairman declined to take a vote on a proposal that someone's next door neighbour should be required to keep her garden tidy.

Last week's annual village meeting at Timberscombe was much more decorous. Timberscombe is a pretty village on the wild and beautiful Exe Valley road between Dunster and Dulverton. I attended it because I happened to be dining with my uncle, a philosopher, who lives in the village. There was a highly intelligent and gifted young official from the County Council to put us all in the picture about a by-pass or through-way to relieve traffic in the village.

It had all started, traditionally enough, with complaints from the Old Age Pensioners. They wanted a special pavement erected so that they could walk through the village without danger from traffic. Nobody would have paid the slightest attention to this if the county highway authority had not discovered that traffic slows to 10 mph in the narrow village street while it negotiates two hairpin bends; this was judged bad for our jet-age image in the county of Butlins and Babycham, so the Council proposed a £50,000 through-way with pavements. Timberscombe might have merited a proper £150,000 by-pass, said the promising young man from the Council, except that in all its five hundred years of history it had never suffered a single road accident; moreover, very few cars use it even in the height of the summer season.

Then the speeches started. Mr Henderson, a brother of the Bishop of Bath and Wells, urged everyone to observe the proprieties of debate, restraining their ugly passions and abiding by the majority decision – keeping it in a *low key* was the memorable phrase he used, no doubt a reference to organ music. He had grave misgivings about the whole scheme.

My uncle, the philosopher, was also sceptical, producing many learned arguments and alternative proposals of great ingenuity. Other speakers took one side or another in gentle, reasoned tones, until suddenly I found myself on my feet declaiming passionately about the dangers of fast traffic. It would be madness, I cried, to allow cars to drive any faster. Timberscombe would become a race-track. Children and old people would be slain in their thousands. In fact, of course, Somerset drivers always behave as if a 30 mph speed limit applied to the whole county, but rhetoric often requires a little embroidery of the facts, and it was all in a good cause. It was a personal triumph when the villagers voted 22–17 against their own request for a traffic improvement scheme.

Examining my own motives, I cannot in honesty claim that I was tremendously concerned about traffic hazards in Timberscombe, but it might have been something to do with

the intelligent young man's take-it-or-leave-it manner. In any case, the outcome was a victory for direct democracy.

Somerset people are being reminded of another experiment in direct democracy by the Church authorities, who have arranged for all the most prominent hills in the county to display three huge crosses throughout this week. Londoners would probably complain at these grisly reminders, being much more concerned about sex and nervous breakdowns, but they should be prepared to suffer a little Biblical exegesis at Easter time.

Listening to the Gospel on Palm Sunday, it struck me that many people criticise Pontius Pilate for his role in the affair while letting the multitude go scot-free. Pilate did what little he could do dissuade them from the extremely unpleasant course of action on which they were set, but the multitude kept shouting for a crucifixion. Pilate could not have done more without provoking a riot. The crucifixion when it happened was a victory for direct democracy against the effete, liberal paternalism of Pilate. This point is underlined when the multitude goes out of its way to say : 'His blood be upon us and upon our children.'

If I am right, and the crucifixion should be seen as an early victory for the principle of direct democracy, then it must follow that one of the messages of Easter, when Christ rose from the dead, is that good men should struggle to confound and frustrate the multitude wherever possible.

Never has there been a message of greater relevance to our own times. It explains Mr Heath's obsession with joining the Common Market against the apparent wishes of the majority and it is a thought which will probably be borne in mind by the old age pensioners of Timberscombe as they skip and jump like mountain goats to avoid the traffic in their village over the Easter weekend.

Join me in my bat hunt...
bring your own bat

Combe Florey, Somerset.
They said there was a very good Italian circus appearing in
Plymouth. I also wanted to collect an interesting photograph
of Lord Gowrie, Mr Heath's exciting new Government
appointment in the House of Lords, from around there. But
when we arrived in West Devon – four children, my dear
wife and I – we learned that one of the trapeze *artistes* had
fallen off her trapeze the day before. This cast a gloom over
the outing, partly out of natural sympathy for the *artiste,*
partly because the trapeze act was sadly incomplete.

It also seemed rather greedy to think about a second
disaster so soon after the first, and it is an unpleasant fact
that however well disposed people feel to the human race at
other times, they only enjoy watching trapeze acts because
there is the risk of an accident. After the show, we went to
see a most distinguished and humane public servant of
pronounced Left-wing views who lives in a castle nearby. He
had been to the circus and said that he did not mind accidents which involved human beings, but couldn't bear the
thought of animals in pain. This provided food for thought on
the seventy-mile journey back to Somerset. Are we approaching the moment for a return of the circuses which were so
popular in Imperial Rome, when Christians were eaten by
lions? They provided vast amusement for the Romans and
obviously kept the lions happy as well.

At least the Church of England seems alive to the possibilities of this new emphasis on animals. Somerset is justly
famous for its magnificent churches, and it is a constant

sadness to Somerset men like myself that these fine buildings have no apparent use in the modern world.

A recent pamphlet produced by the Church Information Office suggests a use for them – as animal and insect sanctuaries. Only inside our churches can furry little creatures like bats, or busy little insects like woodlice, be sure that no one will disturb them as they go about their lawful business of breeding, hanging upside down or eating any oak beams they may find. This is why we should always ask children to be quiet in church. It is also why members of the congregation (in cases where there actually still is a congregation) should not complain about bats' messes on their seats.

I have always been fond of woodlice since I was a boy and we held Woodlouse Derbys. You release a matchbox-full of woodlice in the centre of a segmented circle. The segments are numbered and sold off at a shilling each. The first woodlouse to step out of the circle scoops the pool for the owner of the segment from which he steps out. Since the churches' other great obsession is with raising money they might try to put their woodlice to good use. If the idea of Woodlouse Derbys catches on, the churches might take over from bingo halls as popular centres of entertainment, and no woodlouse need ever again have an anxious thought about the housing situation.

Bats are quite another matter. The report *Wild Life Conservation in the Care of Churches and Churchyards* by G. M. A. Barker, (Church Information Office, 25p), which has a foreword by the Bishop of Leicester, claims that bats are in danger of extinction in the British Isles. This is something I venture to disbelieve, along with the doctrine which maintains that the Queen is supreme head of the Christian Church of England. My own house swarms with bats throughout the summer months. Sometimes I fight them with tennis rackets : sometimes the whole family throws oranges at them as they hang upside down from a picture rail; sometimes we send rat catchers to creep up on them while they are asleep. Nothing makes the slightest bit of difference.

One of the consolations of baldness is that bats can never entangle themselves in your hair. One should never laugh at people like Mr Gerald Kaufman or Mr Patrick Gordon-Walker because they have less hair than Mick Jagger, for instance, or the curly-headed Lord Gowrie, thirty-two, Mr Heath's thrilling new Government appointment. Think how much more useful bald men would be in a bat hunt.

One does not want to provoke a sectarian dispute with the Church of England in this oecumenical age. A compromise must be found. It seems to be that any differences of opinion might be worked off through interdenominational bat hunts. If people find it a strange idea, that those who wish to preserve bats should join those who wish to destroy them in bat hunting, I can only refer them to Hansard's report on the first reading of the Protection of Otters Bill.

Mr Reginald Paget, the wise and kindly Labour member for Northampton, who opposed the Bill, revealed that he was a deep and passionate lover of otters. Like most of us, he is convinced that they do vastly more good than harm. 'If you abolish otter hunting,' he said 'you abolish the one wide-ranging organisation which has an interest in preserving the otter.'

This doctrine seems to open endless possibilities of co-operation between Anglicans and Roman Catholics, bat-lovers and bat hunters, bald and hairy men the world over.

More power to the flowers, I say

La Pesegado, Montmaur, Aude.

Rail strikes are not happy times for those who live in the country. House guests find their stay indefinitely prolonged, which must be worrying for them, and hosts can never enjoy the additional company as fully as they would like if they feel their guests are worried.

We decided to leave Somerset a few days before the go-slow, reckoning we would be in a better position to sympathise with railwaymen among the wild spring flowers of the Languedoc than shivering on the platform of Taunton Station at seven o'clock in the morning.

Ah yes, those poor railwaymen. It must be horrible to live one's life in obedience to a railway timetable. Timetables leave no room for personal expression, for changes of mood or perception, for development of spirit. At least the railwaymen had the sense to take a few days off at this time of year to contemplate the beauties of the season.

The wild flowers down here are quite spectacular; purple

lilac and orchids; cowslips and mustard flowers, wild irises and grape hyacinths, each testifying to the beauty and variety of the world in which we live. The pure sweet air of the Languedoc is quite enough in itself to explain why most forms of work are a crime against nature in springtime. It is a sad feature of our society that no procedure exists for people to take time off work when they feel like it without demanding more money at the same time. Hence the vicious inflationary spiral which threatens to destroy our beautiful capitalist system.

In time, perhaps, people will realise that the greatest benefit of automation is not higher production (of extremely questionable value, anyway) or higher wages for fewer workers. It is that people need only work when they feel like it, or when they need the money.

In France competition is already adjusting itself to a system where absenteeism can be estimated as a seasonal factor. Soon, the free world will accept that factories are only likely to work at full capacity in winter, during a spell of bad weather, or when not much else is going on. I only hope the flowers are still here by the time people come to realise that the Age of Efficiency was all a great mistake.

Our arrival coincided with the great French referendum, so every Frenchman for miles around has felt bound to consult us about British intentions in the Common Market. Whenever we went out, we were inspected from every angle. Are we really the sort of people they want in their nice new Market?

Occasionally, they brought us drinks and asked us searching questions : Why did we want to join? What made us think we would be good members? What did we propose to do about strikes? About Mr Wilson? About Princess Anne?

One evil-smelling old man said he would only vote for British entry if we bought him a drink. We refused. He listened closely while I explained that it was a matter of complete indifference whether we joined or not.

At one time, when it seemed that membership might do something to bring down the murderous price of drink in

England, all patriotic Englishmen were very keen on the idea. There is much to be said for a price structure like that of France, where luxuries like drink are cheap while necessities like food are comparatively expensive. However, since Mr Heath's dream was plainly of an England where everything was expensive, there was no reason why we should help him enrich factory workers in the Midlands, along with their running dogs in the Conservative Party.

If drink was so cheap in France, said this disgusting old man, no doubt we would like to buy him some. Certainly not, I said. Of course, one was mildly in favour of anything which would reduce the sovereignty of the British Parliament, which was altogether excessive. The British House of Commons, I explained, has amongst its members a miserable collection of exhibitionists, social and emotional cripples whose inadequacies gave them some strange compulsion to exert power over other people. Yes, said this crafty man, he had heard that our Parliament was unsatisfactory in many ways, but if we wished anything done about it we would need his vote.

Obviously not all voters are quite such fools as British politicians would have us believe. In France, at least, the peasants know how to put their referendum votes to intelligent use.

But I refused to buy the drunken old brute a drink. Let Mr Heath do his own dirty work. I am not going to spend my hard-earned money bribing French voters on his behalf.

Until he can stir himself to make a clear statement on his policy for the Quantocks, he can expect no financial support from patriotic Englishmen. In any case, such money as the Waugh family apportions to public causes is already earmarked for the Quantock Action Committee whose Treasurer, Mr Michael Kimber (of the Quantock Weaver, Over Stowey, near Bridgwater, Somerset) must pay for a barrister to oppose the disgraceful scheme to allow development of an eighteen-hole championship golf course in the middle of Britain's first area of outstanding natural beauty.

Done out of an honest bob for my squirrels' tails . . .

Combe Florey, Somerset.

Strange and horrible things continue to happen here since Mr Heath's visit to Somerset some weeks ago. At a poultry farm in Bishops Lydeard, where we buy eggs and boiling fowl, the farmer's wife has been plagued by two magpies which carry away her young chickens and devour them at a safe distance before her anguished eyes. These are no day-old chicks so much as young pullets, and nobody has ever seen anything like it before.

Nor, of course, has anyone seen anything like Mr Heath before in Somerset. Conservative party apologists stress that there is no connection between the two events, but I can only say that incidents like these, when magpies behave like roaring lions seeking whom they may devour, do nothing to inspire confidence in the way this country is being run. If

Mr Heath did not want to be held responsible, he should not have made his ill-advised trip.

Confidence in the honesty of government took its hardest knock, at any rate so far as many country folk were concerned, when they stopped paying bounty on squirrels' tails. These tails had to be delivered in bundles of a dozen to qualify for the Government's reward of a shilling a tail, and it often took several years to make up this number. This meant that throughout my schooldays I treasured a number of squirrels' tails in varying stages of decomposition.

They were kept in my bedroom, and at the end of every holiday I counted them against the day I could trade them in at the police station (or post office – I never discovered which) for twelve shillings. Nowadays, of course, 'sixty pee' is less than most children expect to spend on odds and ends every week, before they have even started on sweets or records. But in my deprived childhood, twelve shillings bought seventy cigarettes or thirty-six Mars bars.

My collections of squirrels' tails grew dramatically after the Hungarian uprising of 1956, when a Hungarian forester arrived on the scene. He enjoyed eating the carcasses of squirrels, but had no use for their tails. This was because he was a foreigner and nobody told him of the Government's bounty. But when the great moment arrived and I produced my twelve tails they all laughed in my face and said the Government had changed its policy on squirrels' tails.

My twelve tails weren't worth the bone and gristle which held them together. I threw them away in disgust and dedicated myself from that moment to harassing evil men in high places and to protecting the grey squirrel. But there are many, many farm-houses round here which still keep their sad little bundles of squirrels' tails. They imagine that one day some honest politician will arise who will redeem the Government's promise to pay a shilling a tail, just as people superstitiously kept their Post War Credits, and some still keep their $3\frac{1}{2}$ per cent undated War Loan. At least one can use a squirrel's tail to make the occasional Davy Crockett hat, which is more than one can do with Dalton's $3\frac{1}{2}$ per cents.

Public events have cast a further shadow over Somerset life. One of the great institutions of the countryside is the furniture auction sale. Many people, I should explain, only come to live in the countryside in the autumn of their days. I do not know why this should be so, since towns are probably better equipped to look after the aged. In any case, these senior citizens add much to the life of the country, with their keen interest in other people's affairs and their vigorous complaints about anything which happens.

Just occasionally, however, one of them dies, and then we have a grand furniture auction to commemorate the event. These auctions are attended by all the surviving old people of the neighbourhood, each in search of a souvenir. Ofter they have had their eyes on a particular piece of furniture or china vase, as they met to play bridge of an evening, or to complain about the day's events. Sometimes one spots the same china vase, appearing in house after house in the neighbourhood.

Now this rhythmic cycle has been upset. Local salesrooms are suddenly swarming with blue-chinned figures in berets, reeking of garlic. Junky old desks and armchairs which wouldn't have fetched £5 nine months ago are suddenly fetching £25. Any old rubbish is being loaded into furniture vans and hauled off to France. Secondhand furniture is almost unbelievably expensive over there, as I know to my cost. I also know that it has to pay a hefty tax on arrival in France. Something must be wrong if people can buy this junk in England, cart it across the Channel, pay a hefty tax on arrival and still sell it at a profit. One explanation might be that our own secondhand furniture is too cheap, but I am told that French buyers are now to be seen invading the livestock market in Taunton, buying up all our calves and bullocks as well.

It will be no laughing matter if we lose our entire stock of Edwardian divans and iron-framed pianos. I am thinking particularly of young marrieds, old age pensioners and other worthy people, all of whom have to furnish their houses somehow. Nothing has been made in the past forty years which is not hideous, or over-priced, or both.

The explanation is plainly that our politicians, in their obsession with the balance of payments, have allowed the pound to become seriously under-valued against the franc. Mr Barber should revalue the pound immediately to something nearer its real value of about twenty francs. This matter is fast becoming a national emergency. There is a certain chaise longue in the neighbourhood which I have had my eye on for some time. Its owner, a man of mature years, was looking distinctly peaky the last time I saw him.

To let, Gothic property with extra loud bell (eccentrics welcome)

Combe Florey, Somerset.

May is the month when things begin to happen in the countryside. Already in the past fortnight, the decomposed body of a woman was found on Watchet beach; Kingston St Mary village school held its Sports Day; vandals smashed up the old chapel at Lilstock and destroyed the bells at Dunster; and the *West Somerset Free Press* printed news on its front page for the first time in 112 years. Without this last development I might never have noticed the decomposed corpse on Watchet beach.

Now we should probably expect to see decomposed corpses growing in the fields like mushrooms. News reporting is well known to encourage imitations, which is why television is so dangerous. All media should concentrate on the more wholesome aspects of news.

The Kingston St Mary village school sports day was only a qualified success. Although the sun shone and Miss Daisy Waugh (5) came second (out of three) in the infants' egg-and-spoon race, all other Waugh contestants came in last in every race they entered. Miss Sophia Waugh came last in the ninety yards, the senior girls' egg-and-spoon and the obstacle race; Master Alexander Waugh came last in the same races for boys of his class and also in the sack race; my dear wife came last in the mothers' egg-and-spoon race and I came last in the fathers' race. It was a black day for sport, and also for the instilling of that competitive spirit which is so essential in Mr Heath's England.

People down here have been wondering what Mr Heath intends to do about all these vandals. Vandalism is something which brings out the latent Judge Jeffreys in everyone. No punishment is too bad for people who can smash up beautiful old buildings for no apparent reason, they mutter. Of course, vandals are practically never caught and one seldom has the opportunity of hearing the vandal's point of view. 'Senseless' is the word usually applied to these acts, but when one grasps the simple proposition that vandals obviously enjoy breaking things, then vandalism is no more senseless than playing tennis. So long as beautiful buildings are left empty, vandals will smash them up.

I have some experience of the problem because the property on which I live is approached by a very fine gatehouse dating from 1580 which has been uninhabited for the past hundred years. This was because people always judged it uninhabitable : the living area over the stables, is approached by a high stone spiral staircase; it has no water, or drainage, or electricity, or any of the things which are thought to make life worth living. It stands by the road, and generations of village boys have been unable to resist the temptation of smashing the high mullioned and transomed windows.

As these are of the original diamond pointed and leaded glass, they became very expensive to replace. Finally, with greater prosperity all round, a fairer distribution of wealth, and so on, airgun pellets began to make their appearance in the beautiful Elizabethan plaster ceiling.

A few months ago we decided that something had to be done about it.

For a hundred years the gatehouse had been judged uninhabitable, but nobody had taken into account the eccentricity of the English. Two advertisements – one in *Country Life,* one in *Private Eye* – produced sixty-five applications. Last week a very nice autumnal couple, retired from East Africa, moved in. They will make the house habitable as best they can, and even pay 5p a week for the privilege.

The same remedy would surely apply to all empty churches and chapels which are a permanent temptation to vandals in their present state. One of the saddest aspects of village life

in Somerset, as I often remark on this page, is the plight of the village churches. These magnificent buildings, architecturally the focal point of nearly every village and once its social focus, too, have a forlorn and useless air about them. One might not suppose that many people would want to live in them, climbing up to the belfry every night after cleaning their teeth in the sacristy, but my experience suggests this would be to underestimate the number of eccentrics around.

Vicars would also be well advised to provide alternative smashing facilities for the vandals in their parish. At church fêtes of my youth there was always a side-show called Break up the Happy Home. People brought their cracked china and glass to this stall where would-be vandals paid to be allowed to smash it on the coconut-shy principle. A refinement of this was developed for a church fête in my own home, where visitors were given croquet mallets and balls and invited to aim at a line of bottles. Empty champagne bottles were best. You need to hit them centrally and fairly hard, but the noise was most rewarding.

I have long given up supposing that anyone in authority will ever take up one of my suggestions, but I wish that lawyers and politicians would at least stop crying in baffled rage every time they are confronted by vandalism, reaching for their manual of Nazi war crimes in search of a suitable punishment.

The vicars are almost entirely to blame. If they let retired colonial servants and schoolteachers live in their empty churches, they would not only be protecting the churches from vandals, they would also be making a useful contribution against the national housing shortage. They should also draw attention to the facilities available for smashing things at their church fêtes. Both these suggestions would provide a little money for vicars' living expenses – something their forlorn, vandalised churches are plainly unable to do.

Princess Anne on my doorstep,
but no chance to wave the flag

Combe Florey, Somerset.

Princess Anne visited Somerset last week, spending the entire day at Norton Manor Camp, Norton Fitzwarren, not three miles away from my own home.

For weeks the whole county of Somerset had been told how she would be entertained : various brigadiers and major-generals would be introduced to her – lucky devils! – and she would be shown a Shetland pony only forty inches high; she would be conveyed in a horse-drawn carriage brought specially from Aldershot; a rally of handicapped persons would be held in her honour and she would watch a humorous PT display directed by Sergeant-Major Terry Hammond.

I spent the morning in a frenzy of over-excitement trying to buy Union Jacks in Taunton. All the more respectable shops – drapers, funeral directors, makers of fishing tackle –

treated my inquiry as evidence of some violent intention. At last I found a collection of horrid, plastic flags in a toyshop. Personally, I would hesitate to wave them at Lady Sarah Armstrong-Jones, but the children seized on them eagerly.

Sophisticated Londoners may find this enthusiasm strange, but they should remember that country-dwellers have not had the same opportunity to watch Princess Anne develop. I think I saw her many years ago at the Badminton Horse Trials but if so she was only a slip of a thing and it might well have been Prince Richard of Gloucester. This was my first opportunity to see her in all the glory and pride of young womanhood.

Moreover, Somerset increasingly resembles a geriatric institution as more and more senior citizens settle here for the autumn of their days. Princess Anne could scarcely fail to draw a crowd for her youth, even without her august lineage and picturesque associations.

So we went to Norton Manor Camp with our Union Jacks at the ready. Norton Manor is widely revered in the neighbourhood as being the probable birthplace of Douglas Woodruff, the great Roman Catholic editor and biographer of the Tichborne Claimant. Nowadays it houses the Junior Leaders' Regiment of the Royal Corps of Transport.

At the gates we were stopped by two rather goofy Junior Leaders who demanded the password, or pass, or something like that. We replied – perhaps a trifle airily – that we were members of the public who had come to see Princess Anne. Not without a Passover, or by-pass, or passport, said the Junior Leader, who had obviously decided I was some sort of trade unionist. We protested that many members of the public had been waiting sixteen years for a glimpse of Princess Anne in her prime. The Junior Leader's lip curled. There were no facilities for members of the public to contemplate Her Royal Highness, he said. We said we would wait outside the camp and wave our flags when she emerged in the evening. For the first time the Junior Leader smiled. Her Royal Highness was leaving by helicopter, you see.

Of course, it is no part of my purpose to criticise Royalty.
I am a religious man myself, although belonging to a different
persuasion. But I do think that those responsible for Royal
arrangements might have been a little more considerate.
Somerset folk have just as much curiosity about these things
as anyone else, and some of the speculation one hears about
Princess Anne down here strikes me as ill-informed. Nobody
denies that Princess Anne is at present in the full flower of
her youth. My only point is that these things fade :

Golden lads and girls all must

As chimney sweepers, come to dust.

Through mismanagement and bureaucratic incompetence,
the hardworking villagers of Norton Fitzwarren, Bishops
Lydeard, Halse and Combe Florey may have lost their only
opportunity of seeing Princess Anne in her prime. Which
brings into question the whole purpose of sending this conscientious young lady down to the West Country, if she was
not to be exposed to the public gaze.

If she only wanted to make a personal pilgrimage to the
birthplace of Douglas Woodruff, there was no need for all
the advance publicity. In any case, it would have been easier
for her to visit that good and wise man in his own home, near
Abingdon – a stone's throw from Windsor compared to Norton Fitzwarren. The official explanation that she came all this
way to meet some soldiers, is, like so many official explanations, the least plausible of all. Both London and Windsor
are crammed with soldiers, if ever Princess Anne wishes to
meet them. Admittedly the dress and behaviour of some
Guardsmen may be a trifle unconventional but that is no
reason for helicopter excursions to West Somerset.

Mr Willie Hamilton, Labour MP for West Fife, will probably want to know how much the Army spent from the
national defence budget on sending a horse-drawn vehicle from
Aldershot to Norton Fitzwarren. Its purpose was to carry
the Princess from the parade ground to the officers' mess for
lunch, a distance of some yards. No members of the public
were allowed to watch this curious ceremony, so it can

scarcely have helped recruitment or improved the Army's image in the world at large.

But what really rankles is that this secret pageant should be staged in Somerset, where we motor twenty miles for a cinema, eighty for a circus – and only three miles from my own front door.

My explanation is that someone in Princess Anne's entourage read about Mr Heath's controversial visit to Weston-super-Mare and hoped by sending the Princess down here to bring the two together. Hence the exclusion of the public, and hence the elaborate smoke-screen of humorous PT displays.

Alas, she was several weeks too late and some thirty miles off target.

It is not my place to bring the two together but surely there is someone in London who can ask them both to tea – Mark Boxer, perhaps, or Lady Hartwell. There is no excuse for inflicting these strange courting rituals on honest West Countrymen.

Be warned before you come out West

Combe Florey, Somerset.

First summer sunshine has a curious effect on the West Country. The roads are suddenly alive and vibrant with motor cars hooting at each other through clouds of exhaust as they crawl bumper to bumper at ten miles an hour, always in the same direction.

Taking the children to the North Cornish seaside for the day one had the impression of joining some epic migration, like the Jewish Diaspora, the Great Trek of the Boers from Cape Province or Mao's Long March.

Of course it is really nothing more than our fellow Britishers having a good time. Every car carries a polythene bundle on its roof-rack until the procession resembles an army of ants with eggs on their backs. It is a beautiful thing, of course, that people who pass their working lives earning money in the noise and hideousness of the West Midlands should choose to spend their holidays motoring very slowly in procession past my gate.

On the other hand, I am not sure that if I were a Midlands car worker I should venture into the West Country at this particular moment when meat is so expensive. As I mentioned a few weeks ago, all the heavily subsidised British meat which comes into the market down here is immediately snapped up by Frenchmen who take it away with many greedy noises to eat in their own country.

Many West Countrymen are feeling meat-deprived and there have been ugly rumours of cannibalism.

We cannot know if this is what Mr Heath had in mind when he started his new style of government, but people intending to take their holiday in the West Country should

be warned. Many visitors who come to us from Wolverhampton and Coventry – we try to make them welcome –
seem so weighed down by all the money in their pockets
that they can scarcely walk, let alone run. The best
they can manage is a sedate, jingling waddle from the
car to the nearest public convenience. It would be a sad
and rather shocking thing is at the end of the holiday season
these public conveniences were surrounded by the whitened
bones of holidaysmakers, picked clean by scavenging
natives.

Another effect of the sun has been to turn all the milk sour.
At least I suppose we must blame the sun, although we are
often told how the modern farmer treats his milk in a centri-
fugal atomiser, bombards it with electronic particles and
flambés it in paraffin until it can't possibly turn sour in the
sun. Day after day we parents swear that nothing is wrong
with milk which smells and tastes of goat cheese. Obviously
one cannot go on indefinitely blaming all misfortunes on Mr
Heath's ill-advised visit to Somerset some months ago. But
I must report that there is growing uncertainty down here
about whether Mr Heath is quite the right man for his
present job.

For instance, his Government has suddenly decided to put
up huge signs in yellow and black enamel every mile or so
along all the main roads of Devon, Somerset and Cornwall.
They display the letters HR and must have cost at least £6
each, but nobody has any idea what they mean. The only
other place where I have seen these letters was on the roof
of the Old Library, at Christ Church, Oxford. There they
refer to King Henry VIII of evil memory, the cruel and repul-
sive despot so unlike our present Queen.

Diligent enquiry reveals that the letters stand for Holiday
Route, but even if holidaymakers knew this it is fatuous to
suppose they would pay any attention to it; they all want to
go to different places, you see. Goodness knows how many
hundreds of thousands of pounds have been spent on this
futile enterprise.

The picture is scarcely more cheerful with the Williton and Dunster Association. A massive headline in the *West Somerset Free Press* – far and away the best newspaper in England – proclaimed 'Despondency Lurks Over the Williton and Dunster Association.' The story underneath gave chapter and verse to this lurid claim : 'Gloomy despondency hung over the Williton and Dunster Association's annual meeting at the Egremont Hotel, Williton, on Wednesday last week. Six members turned up to hear the hon. secretary, Mr Jack Newton, complain : "Apathy has reared its ugly head in no small measure – particularly among our former members".'

Is this what Mr Heath meant when he promised us a quiet revolution? But the real test of the present Government's sincerity will come next Tuesday when a public enquiry opens in Taunton to determine the future of the Quantocks.

The immediate issue concerns 250 acres at the centre of the hills. These acres were 'reclaimed' – most mistakenly – into indifferent agricultural land three years ago with the help of an enormous subsidy from the Government. The owner has now been offered a large sum of money to turn them into an eighteen-hole championship golf course which will dominate the hills with access roads and other amenities, effectively turning the Quantocks into an adjunct of the golf course – the Quantocks where Wordsworth and Coleridge first discovered the beauties of the English countryside and introduced Southey, Lamb, De Quincey and Hazlitt to the daring idea that nature can be beautiful.

This idea has not yet got through to Somerset County Council, who are supporting the golf course, even though there is already a perfectly good one three and a half miles away at Enmore.

What makes the Quantock hills so exceptional nowadays – and of concern to those who live outside the area – is that very few roads go through them. They are one of the very few places in southern England where people can get away from the motor car to enjoy surroundings of outstanding natural beauty.

Needless to say there is a scheme – warmly supported by local government bodies – to build a spine road along their top and make them part of the great Exmoor driverama. We shall discuss the bold idea later, but the battle against the golf course is now entering a crucial phase. It would be a very good time for anyone who knows and loves the Quantocks to write, telephone or call on the Secretary of State for the Environment at 3 Marsham Street, S.W.1. I know Mr Walker would be most grateful for advice on this matter.

Take a brolly to combat Captain

Combe Florey, Somerset.

Last week the neighbouring village of Bishop's Lydeard held its annual carnival. There can be little doubt that these jamborees date from some pre-Christian fertility festival. Almost everything in the countryside can be explained in terms of the fertility cult and there was certainly a new, slightly sinister note of militancy this year, with all the talk of a population policy.

'Never mind the Common Market, join the Bishop's Lydeard Carnival,' said one banner.

At moments this pastoral frolic seemed closer to a Nuremberg rally. A grand procession of carnival floats was headed by the massed band of the Junior Leaders' Regiment from Norton Fitzwarren and followed by the Kingsbury Episcopi Brass Band, many of whose members wore dinner jackets.

My suspicions of the Bishop's Lydeard Carnival date from four years ago when I entered my youngest daughter, Daisy, for the baby competition, sponsored by a powdered milk firm. It is embarrassing to have to ask my readers to take it on trust, but everybody who saw her agrees that Daisy Waugh was one of the most beautiful babies they have ever seen. When we put her down on the beach at Minehead, a crowd of about forty-five people gathered round her basket in a matter of minutes. When we left her for a few days at a farm near Dulverton, people came from miles around to see her and one old lady, nearly blind and approaching ninety, walked on foot all the way from a neighbouring village to catch what can only, alas, have been a glimpse. Daisy was as brown as a hazelnut with a smile to melt the cruellest judge's heart, but the judges at the Bishop's Lydeard Baby Show did not give her a second glance.

For my own part I will never buy that particular brand
of powdered milk again. The baby which won looked more
like a pig than a human child. It might as well have been
a pig, in fact – as I learned afterwards that babies were
judged only on size, like vegetable marrows, with no marks
for beauty or wit or sweetness of character. This strikes me as
extremely irresponsible. There is no need to fatten babies like
turkeys for eating, and obesity is one of the major childhood
afflictions nowadays, like scarlet fever fifty years ago. Eating
sweets does more harm to the quality of life in Britain than all
the poisons pouring out of our factories. Sometimes I receive
letters complaining that frogs or larks or hedgehogs are no
longer to be found where once they danced and sang and
waddled.

But nature, by and large, has a resilience which children's
teeth quite plainly lack. There are more larks around Combe
Florey than we have any use for, and anyone is welcome to
come and catch some. Similarly, we have a plague of wood-
peckers at the moment, although it is true to say that the frog
population has declined.

This has nothing to do with the activities of Rio Tinto
Zinc at Avonmouth, or with the French hydrogen bomb tests.
It is because they have all been eaten by a goose called Captain which lives on an island in the lake below my house.
At one time all the lanes around would be carpeted with
squashed frogs throughout the summer – a sad sight and also
rather unpleasing for those of delicate or refined tastes. Nowadays one rarely meets so much as a tadpole.

Captain belonged for many years to a gardener who died
two years ago. Nobody came to claim the goose, so he has
stayed on, attacking everybody who walks up the drive and
often attacking visitors' cars. Nobody will mind in the
slightest bit when he dies, and he seems to sense this, attacking
even people who go to feed him with crusts of bread and
stale loaves. As a result, he relies mostly on a diet of frogs,
which may be what makes him bad-tempered, like the French.

Incidentally, the best defence against a savage goose is an

umbrella, which you open in his face as he runs at you. This will not frighten him – a really angry goose scarcely knows the meaning of fear – but it diverts his fury. Geese are stupid enough to attack the umbrella instead of the person who carries it.

He is also a sentinel of sorts. I like to think of the havoc he will cause among the Junior Leaders' Military Band from Norton Fitzwarren, if they ever try marching up my drive in the event of a military takeover. This seems more likely than ever after the Bishop's Lydeard Carnival: there is an ugly spirit moving in the land. Addressing the public inquiry into the proposed championship golf course in Taunton last week, I was surprised and dismayed to find myself on the crest of a great popular wave. For some reason, the idea of stopping this golf course has really caught the popular imagination and for the first time I began to understand what it is that makes people like Mussolini, Castro and Mr Eldon Griffiths go into politics.

When a local landowner called Major T. E. Trollope-Bellew rose to speak in favour of the golf course, many people present honestly thought he was going to be lynched.

God help us all, but I have a feeling that those who try to inflict further changes on the country at this particular moment in time will be unleashing forces which we will all live to regret.

Roast hedgehog anyone?

Tonbridge, Kent.
July might seem a good month to visit the fruit and hop farms of rural Kent, but for peace and quiet you would do better to join the Orange celebrations in Derry commemorating the Battle of the Boyne. This is because of the new technology of bird scaring, probably a spin-off from the moon programme, the Vietnamese war, Concorde and all the other exciting and wonderful ways which governments have found for spending our money.

A huge cherry orchard I found near the village of Tudeley would be an ideal place for inspiring gloom and significant thoughts in people like Chekhov except for the bangs. At irregular intervals, and without any warning, any of about fifteen little blue machines on the ground will explode with a terrific noise – certainly greater than the twenty-pounder tank guns I used to let off on National Service whenever the Government decided it had some money which needed

spending. Goodness knows how these machines work, but they could easily be miniaturised, domesticated, washable atom bombs. I have often noticed that rational people lose all sense of proportion when they feel threatened by birds and small animals : squirrels, rabbits, sparrows, bullfinches, all seem to bring out the Doctor Strangelove lurking behind so many simple, red, agricultural faces.

Before China had the atom bomb, Mao ordered all the able-bodied men, women and children in the length and breadth of the land to go out of doors and clap their hands to frighten the birds. His idea was that the birds would all die of exhaustion as they fluttered in terror from clapping China-man to clapping Chinaman. Then I suppose they planned to eat all the little birds' nests in a last great feast. This is what somebody once told me. If true, it shows Mao as being stupid as well as cruel. How could he be sure that the birds would die of exhaustion before their tormentors? He would have looked very silly if he was left with 630 million dead China-men and some tired, resentful sparrows to rule over.

My reason for this long disquisition about Mao's treat-ment of little birds is that our own Government, in its own small way, is beginning to try exactly the same policy against gipsies. Kent is still swarming with them, although farmers tell me they prefer machinery for their hop and fruit-picking nowadays, as being cheaper and less argumentative.

I saw heavy concentrations of gipsies around Orpington and Chislehurst, all apparently engaged in the scrap metal trade, and it was easy to see why some local people object to them as neighbours.

I have never been able to feel great sentimental attraction towards the gipsy life, even if they do know how to roast hedgehogs in a clay envelope which removes the prickles when opened. My father claimed to have done this as a Boy Scout, and I was never able to decide whether he was telling the truth or whether he was joking, as it is called when grown-ups tell a lie. I have told exactly the same story to my children about myself, and always chuckle inwardly as I tell it. I did many disgusting and shameful things as a Boy Scout, but I never ate a hedgehog.

Many aspects of the gipsy life are undeniably anti-social, and I can easily understand those London and County Boroughs who wish to discourage further gipsies once they have provided the site for fifteen gipsy caravans as they are required to do under the Caravan Sites Act of 1968. What I cannot understand, and what makes no sense outside the logic of Mao Tse Tung's bird solution, is why the central government has started encouraging London and County Boroughs to harass gipsies instead of providing more sites for them.

The penalties in Mr Lubbock's Act were meant to encourage gipsies to use these sites every bit as much as they were intended to discourage excessive concentrations of gipsies. The Department of the Environment now seeks to use these penalties to promote the spine-chilling concept of 'surplus' gipsies who can be harassed from County Borough to County Borough until they end up in prison.

Far more annoying than gipsies – at any rate in my experience – are gipsy lovers. They, too, have an unpleasing way of distinguishing between 'proper' gipsies – that is racially pure Romanies – and didikois, or half breeds, for whom no fate is bad enough. This seems no less odious to me than the Government's distinction between gipsies for whom camp sites have been provided and 'surplus' gipsies. If the politicians wish to harass someone they should harass all caravan users and not only those who have no other homes.

My own part of the country – West Somerset and North Devon – is made very nearly uninhabitable at this time of the year by holidaymakers who insist on bringing their caravans with them. They make the countryside they have come to enjoy hideous with their caravan parks and they block the narrow, winding roads until it sometimes takes two hours to cover the seven miles to Taunton for shopping. A simple law banning caravans from all roads except motorways would solve the problem.

The great purpose of caravans, I suppose, is to save a few

pounds on bed and breakfast, thereby destroying a means of livelihood for many country dwellers and denying most of them any benefit from the invasion. They also help depress the abysmal standard of British hotels, discourage tourism and probably prejudice our entire foreign exchange position. At any rate, Somerset holds no allure for the next six weeks so we are escaping to France, where we shall spend some of Mr Barber's precious reserves of foreign currency.

Through the smoke — that's M. Wang

La Pesegado, Montmaur, Aude.

The countryside has an entirely different meaning for French people – partly, I expect, because there is so much more of it in France. Rather than something to be sighed over and preserved, it is a boring obstacle to be covered at maximum speed between huge meals. Obviously, French eating habits create stupendous problems of garbage disposal – and the only answer is to dump it all in the countryside.

On our journey south we passed many, many signs warning us about the dangers of alcohol, but none urging us to keep France tidy. However, my dear wife, who was brought up near Guildford in Surrey and has good suburban instincts, was determined to keep France tidy whether they like it or not. The remains of every picnic were preserved in the car like sacred relics – rancid butter, stinking cheese, rotten peaches, stale bread and sad, bad pieces of *paté* – until we might find a litter bin. Needless to say, there was not a single litter bin to be found between Le Havre and Chenonceaux, 200 miles to the south.

Chenonceaux, whose beautiful Italianate château designed by Trinqueau in 1513 spans the River Cher on five magnificent arches, is now entirely devoted to the tourists. Litter bins are provided as an additional tourist attraction, catering especially for the strange tastes of visiting English. When we arrived, in a swarm of flies and bringing a terrible smell with us, we filled three litter bins with what we had saved, watched sourly by an old gardener. No doubt it was his job to empty the little bins and spread the rubbish over the countryside where it belonged.

At La Pesegado, our determination to keep France tidy

caused even greater havoc. There is no dustbin collection within miles of our farm. Country people are expected to empty their dustbins in a little heap outside their house where the growing pile of snail shells and poor, legless frogs' carcasses serves as something of a status symbol, in addition to its obvious ornamental value. For our own part, we tip our rubbish into a small quarry about a hundred yards from the house and burn it when the wind is blowing away.

On the second day of our arrival I lit the mouldering heap in the time-honoured way of pouring meths over it and throwing matches from a safe distance. However, I had misjudged the occasion and soon the entire countryside was burning, garbage and all. Feeling a little foolish, I stared in dismay while the children ran backwards and forwards from the house with toothmugs of water. Meanwhile, my wife drove off to the nearest telephone, about three miles away, and summoned the immediate aid of Castelnaudary's noble fire brigade.

We live about a mile from the nearest public road through a complicated maze of farm tracks and ancient Roman ways, about ten miles from the market town of Castelnaudary, famous for its bean stew called cassoulet and its eighteenth-century windmill. It is also famous for its Fire Brigade under the courageous Captain Réné Peytavy, who doubles as the

municipal engineer. Somehow those brave, intelligent men found the way, but when they arrived to British cheers and loud about half an hour later, the fire had gone out.

Feeling a little embarrassed I hid behind a tree and pretended to be reading a rubbishy novel about Sir Walter Raleigh, leaving my wife to engage them in conversation. Seeing that the fire was out, Captain Peytavy himself congratulated her on the promptness with which she had summoned assistance. His twelve assistants drew a hose out of the fire engine and poured 2,000 litres of water on the surrounding countryside to demonstrate what they would have done if there had been a fire.

The *pompiers* brought with them a journalist from the local newspaper, *L'Indépendant* of Perpignan. He was a sort of Graham Greene character in the natty suiting of an earlier age, and obviously made a habit of following Castelnaudary Fire Brigade. My wife, for some feminine reason or other, treated him with suspicion and hesitated even to confide her name. Perhaps she mistook him for one of those ghouls who enliven the scene of every disaster in England. At any rate, he took great offence and said he could easily find it out by inquiring in the neighbourhood.

The story appeared a few days later with a photograph extending across three columns, captioned thus: 'While awaiting the firemen, M Oberon Wang had tried to put out the fire. In our picture, he holds a bucket in his hand; at the extreme left Mme Wang, who speaks French, is entertaining herself with an inhabitant of Montmaur.'

The article concluded with a tribute to the exemplary devotion with which the Castelnaudary Fire Brigade always carries out its tasks: 'Let us give homage to all the engineer-pumpers of Castelnaudary under the direction of their Captain Réné Peytavy. . . .'

I was a little nervous in case the fire brigade made an enormous charge for its services but I need not have worried. Very few things in France are free, but the authorities are worried that nobody will ever call the Fire Brigade if they make a charge.

Last Easter I thought that English prices were beginning to catch up with the French, but since Mr Barber's brilliant decision to float the pound everything is much more expensive again in France, at any rate for English people. If visitors find themselves running short of money and wish to pass a most instructive afternoon entirely free of charge they should remember Captain Peytavy's words: *The Fire Brigade is always happy to be of service.*

The mystery of the angel with four big toes

La Pesegado, Montmaur, Aude.

This August will obviously be remembered as the Summer of the Strange Footprints. It may seem incredible that while the newspapers go rambling on about a seventy-stone monster called Big Foot in the forests of British Columbia, something much more sinister has been sitting on our very doorstep in southern France. We learned about it at lunch with our neighbour, a farmer.

He is a friendly soul who very much enjoys conversation: unfortunately, as he talks in a mixture of *patois* and the heavily-accented French of the Midi, it is seldom possible to understand much of what he says. This does not worry him, but it is disconcerting for the listener who has to guess whether he is telling an amusing anecdote about some rabbits or describing the death of someone very dear to him. He is a

kind man, without any malice or guile, and one would not like to make a mistake. Towards the end of a very long lunch, I came to realise that he had been telling us once again the story of the Pesegado. Attentive readers will remember that the name Pesegado means a footprint in the *patois* of the Languedoc. In the mists of history, it would appear, an angel landed on the hillside and left its footprint in the rock; the footprint remained there until the summer of 1947 when the farmer grew bored with it and blew it up with dynamite.

Since writing that story, I have heard a slightly different version of it from the Mayor of Montmaur, who is something of a historian. Far from it being an angel, he claims it was Our Lady herself who landed on the hillside – and the event was commemorated for many years by a chapel which stood on the site of our farm called Notre Dame de Pezegade. Travellers along the ancient cart track in times gone by would pause to worship the stone or receive wholesome vibrations from it or whatever. Later, presumably, local farmers grew bored with having the chapel there and blew it up; in any case, all accounts agreed that the Pesegado itself had been destroyed soon after the war.

My guest favoured the version that it had been Our Lady who had landed on the hillside so many years ago. In this he was supported by his wife, who had seen the footprint often, and testified that it was much more like the Blessed Virgin's footmark than that of a mere angel.

However, when the old man came to the end of the story, we began to notice a significant difference. He had been present when the outrage was committed twenty-five years ago, and spoke of it as quite a jolly occasion. But there was no mention of dynamite. Under a sudden barrage of questions, he admitted that there had been several of them present and they had merely tipped the rock over a cliff down the side of the mountain. Was it still there? He supposed he could find it.

So it was after rather a heavy lunch that our expedition set off in search of extra-territorial footprints. There was myself, my youngest brother, Septimus Waugh, a Bachelor of

Arts of Oxford University, the old farmer and his son. We were armed only with sticks and a crowbar, and we had to pause from time to time to allow the old gentleman to relieve himself, but we found the Pesegado without difficulty. It lay half buried in earth on the scorched mountainside where it had lain all those years since being tipped there by a group of over-excited and probably tipsy farmers.

My brother Septimus made the first disquieting discoveries. He was almost certainly the first Oxford BA to have set eyes on the footprint and he noticed immediately that it had four big toes and three little ones.

As if this was not horrible enough, he also noticed that the footprint was 36 inches long. According to Mr Adrian Berry, the *Sunday Telegraph's* expert on footprints, who cites Professor Philip Tobias, of Witwatersrand University, as his authority the length of a human foot is about fifteen per cent of total stature. This would make the Virgin Mary twenty feet high. By comparison, the Big Foot monster which the *Sunday Times* had been pursuing in British Columbia is only ten feet high.

If future generations, with the mystery of Stonehenge and the Pyramids in mind, wish to know how this huge stone came to be moved back to its original position, the answer is that my brother Septimus and I managed to manoeuvre it into the boot of a car and drive it up the mountainside. Not many Englishmen would have attempted the task without a very heavy lunch beforehand.

Where be all this permissiveness?

Combe Florey, Somerset.
The great Poetry Celebration at Nettlecombe, near Stogumber, was Somerset's answer to the Woodstock Pop Festival of some years ago. Nettlecombe is a large and beautiful mansion which belongs to a painter, John Wolseley. Last week he decided for one reason or another to import a gaggle of poets at great expense from Liverpool, London and Ulster.

Beautiful, doe-eyed women appeared from nowhere to stare goofily at them and that, basically, was the Celebration. Stogumber had seen nothing like it, at any rate, since the marriage of Sir Francis Drake to Elizabeth Sydenham in 1585.

There were no scenes of depravity at the Poetry Celebration, but then not very many people turned up for it. Peter Hesp, chief feature writer of the *Somerset County Gazette*, uncovered a single, alleged case of what he described

as tipsiness at a cricket match between the poets and a visiting team. He is a former lay preacher and also, as it happens, a poet. The only other excitement was when somebody threw a bottle. This came during a long harangue, delivered to the local Somerset landowners and these strange, goofy girls by a coloured group called the Third World Troubadors, all about the advantages of Black Power and World Revolution. Everybody cheered enthusiastically, and of course we were all quite prepared to hold a race riot or a world revolution or whatever was expected of us, but there somehow didn't seem quite enough people present to see it through.

And that is one of the main problems of living in Somerset. We hear politicians and saloon bar Napoleons talking about how England is bursting at the seams with coloured immigrants and sexual permissiveness, but none of it ever seems to get down to Somerset. I used to see an African family in church at Wiveliscombe about fifteen miles away, and there are some very nice Chinese restaurateurs in Taunton. Dr David Owen, the bright young Labour MP for one of the Plymouth constituencies, was in Bridgwater last week publicly urging Ugandan Asians to come and settle in the West Country. He said we should receive them with 'discretion, modesty, openness and generosity,' which is a very beautiful way of putting it.

They might also do something to discourage the invading white hordes from Wolverhampton, Birmingham and the West Midlands, who make West Somerset uninhabitable every summer. But I doubt whether many of them will pay much attention to him.

Of course one does not wish to use emotive language about the people from Wolverhampton who pour up and down the A38 throughout the summer holidays like gases in a chemical retort. Their accents may be difficult to understand and they may cook unspeakable things in the billy-cans they bring with them. Over and above all that, as Mr Powell constantly points out, it is a question of numbers. But we are all members of the great human family, and in any case most Somerset men have been able to get away from the invasion – at any rate for as long as our school holidays coincided.

And this, of course, is where the Education Committee of the Somerset County Council has to step in. According to a brilliant new educational theory they have worked out, all school time which is not spent preparing for a specific examination is time wasted. So instead of having an idle period after the exams when our Children can cultivate what are laughingly called their minds, they are going to be sent home three weeks earlier, and return to work before the August Bank Holiday. Somerset parents are therefore going to be imprisoned here for three weeks while the rest of the world goes on holiday, drives down to Sunny Somerset and blocks the roads for eighty miles in every direction.

At the same time we learn that this may be no more than a two-year pilot scheme for something far, far worse : the four-term year. If this comes about, it will mean that our children have holidays in June and September but will be at school throughout July and August. Nobody has yet worked out exactly what are the advantages of this new arrangement, if any, nor how Somerset will fit in with the rest of the country's examination schedules, but the general feeling is one of modest pride in another First for Somerset.

But there is a much better solution which has been working in France for many years. They have huge children's holiday camps, called *colonies de vacances,* heavily subsidised by the government, where children are sent unaccompanied, so that their parents can go on holiday without them. In France, at least, the children seem to have the time of their lives.

It may be argued that normal English children are much too tender, or too wet, or too sensitive, or whatever, to allow themselves to be sent away from home unaccompanied. My own observation leads me to believe that in many cases this objection may, indeed, be true, but what the eye does not see the heart does not grieve about and parents should comfort themselves that the experience will almost certainly do their kiddies some good.

Obviously, the best place to put these holiday camps is in West Somerset. Whatever one may say against children, at least they don't drive cars. If they succeed in keeping their parents away they will have achieved much more than any number of Ugandan Asians could hope to do.

Come on in — the squeeze is lovely!

Combe Florey, Somerset.

The Chairman of Porlock Parish Council is called James Bond. Like the young Winston Churchill, Conservative MP for Stretford, he it not one to be cowed by the weight of his famous name.

James Bond of Porlock presents a vigorous, fighting front to the world, and last Tuesday he lashed out at 'certain newcomers' who were obstructing development in Porlock. He referred to the previous week's parish meeting where, he claimed, residents tried to dictate the type of houses to be built on Porlock's allotment field.

'There was more said by people who have only lived here a twelve-month than by anyone else,' thundered Porlock's 007. 'They come here and don't want anyone else to move in.'

Perhaps I should explain the background. Porlock is a pretty village on the edge of Exmoor. It once had its own harbour, but the sea has receded to Porlock Weir, and the village itself is chiefly remembered nowadays by the fact that it was a person from Porlock who interrupted Coleridge when he was in the middle of composing 'Kubla Khan', with the result that we shall never know what the damsel with a dulcimer would have done next. Porlock's other claim to fame is that the poet Southey was once stranded in the old Ship Inn by a rainstorm and was so desperately bored that he had to write a sonnet about the experience:

'*Porlock! I shall forget thee not*
Here by the unwelcome summer rain confined . . .
Making my sonnet by the alehouse fire,
Whilst Idleness and Solitude inspire

Dull rhymes to pass the duller hours away.

This view was not at all shared by Mrs Ida Down (literally : unless this is all an elaborate joke by the staff of the *West Somerset Free Press,* James Bond's supporter was called Mrs Ida Down). She testified that 'Porlock is about the best place to live.'

She argued that it would be a selfish attitude to try and keep others away. 'I like living here and like other people to come and enjoy it as well,' averred Mrs Ida Down.

And so the battle rages. Porlock, as I have said, is a pretty village, but its chief glory lies in the countryside around – Selworthy Beacon above it on one side and on the other the famous cliff-top road to Lynton and Lynmouth which must be one of the most beautiful coast drives in England, if not Europe.

The Great Debate over what sort of bungalows are to be built in Porlock's three-acre allotment field has only arisen because it concerns parish property. Normally a bungalow will spring up like a mushroom, almost over-night, as soon as planning permission is granted and a retired bank manager from Solihull will be sitting by the fire in his bedroom slippers before you can say 'Jack Robinson'. In this case, not only are all the gas-bags of the village entitled to give their opinion,

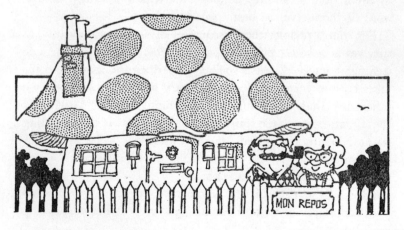

but also the Department of the Environment's approval must be given and this, I am delighted to say, has not yet happened.

The general rule for countryside planning is that new buildings will only be permitted if they can be described as 'in-filling'. This strange word embraces the doctrine that any atrocity can be put up inside a village so long as it does not impinge on the empty spaces around. It's justification lies in the palpably false belief that country villages are still organic communities rather than retirement centres for the urban aged.

In any case, all our villages will soon be 'in-full,' but the application of this doctrine has already meant that practically every village of West Somerset has had its character completely changed by a number of post-war retirement bungalows squeezed into any available patch of land within the village precincts. The fact that these bungalows are, almost without exception, of a hideousness which has to be seen to be believed is only incidental to the Great Debate. Nor, of course, is there the slightest reason why people should not retire to our national parks, if they wish to. What the Great Debate of Porlock Parish Council is really about, it seems to me, is whether our national parks should be earmarked and exploited as retirement areas for the elderly, like the Red Indian reservations of Arizona, Oklahoma and Wyoming, or whether they should be earmarked, as they theoretically are, as areas of outstanding beauty into which settling old folk must fit themselves as best they can.

For many people, the destruction of such rural beauty as survives is a small price to pay for this. Guilt over the vile treatment which English society prescribes for its old people takes curious forms : a local dignitary solemnly proposed the other day that the county should build a spine road over the Quantocks – the only remaining area of outstanding natural beauty unspoiled by the motor car – because very old people, who can no longer walk are unable to enjoy the Quantocks without such a road.

Obviously a decision on whether to preserve the national parks as places of beauty for all ages or whether to develop them as geriatric reservations must soon be made, one way or the other.

If the matter is left to local councils, they will become bungalow conurbations within the next fifteen years, and the same, I am sorry to say, seems true of the various national park committees which appear to have fallen into the hands of local landowners and profiteers. Whether Mr Peter Walker is a man of sufficient calibre to take on all these vested interests and save the countryside remains to be seen.

We still await his decision on the proposal to take over a commanding central stretch of the Quantocks as an eighteen-hole championship golf course.

How to make the growing great...

Combe Florey, Somerset.

The news that British Rail is planning to close down the direct rail link between London and the West Country caused a certain amount of despondency down here. Under the new proposals, anyone wishing to visit Taunton and points west must go on an enormous loop almost into Oxford, passing through Didcot and Swindon, Bristol, Weston-super-Mare and Bridgwater before reaching Taunton.

This brilliant innovation would add – at present speeds – about an hour and a half to the journey and make London farther away than Taunton, in time, than it has been since the middle of the nineteenth century, it would do so, that is, if anyone continued to travel by train. There is much to be said for turning the clock back in this way, of course, except that there is no corresponding proposal to cut us off from the West Midlands and the North.

Last week I visited Blackpool where most hotels serve their evening meal – a four-course affair involving cream of chicken soup, creamed potatoes, creamed turkey and brussels sprouts, sherry trifle with artificial cream – at five o'clock. The management has to play gramophone records at diners before they can eat it. Yet this is what the customers like, and if the West Country is to settle down as the playground of the North, I fear this is what we will have to learn to do.

But the most immediate effect of these leaked proposals has been to undermine confidence in Government management yet again. Listening to angry demands for the nationalisation of land at the Labour Party Conference last week, I could not help feeling an infinite pity for the poor cows and sheep which will have to live on the land afterwards.

At least one proposal at Blackpool should give the West Country a little hope for the future. It came from Mr Denis Howell, who never struck me as a particularly inspiring Minister of Sport in Mr Wilson's government. He demanded that the retirement age for men should be reduced to sixty as a matter of urgent social priority.

Anybody who lives in one of the country's retirement areas will know exactly what he means. At present, as I sometimes mention, the people who come down here in the autumn of their lives to build themselves a bungalow or two and complain about the way life has treated them are often, tragically, a little too old to add much to the general vitality of the region. Even their complaints somehow lack zip. With a new injection of vivacious, sixty-year-old pensioners and their bright-eyed fun-loving wives we can reopen all our village schools (long since closed for want of children) as protest centres and have dancing on the village greens again.

For the moment, however, all feeling is strongly against the Government. At Dulverton Rural Council meeting last Friday they laughed aloud at a letter from the Rural District Councils' Association suggesting various ways to celebrate Britain's entry into the Common Market. Amid ribald comments they decided to take no action. Watchet Urban Council has declined to accept Ugandan refugees on the grounds of a shortage of jobs.

Nether Stowey pleads that it is too 'close-knit' as a village, as well as having a housing shortage 'I don't think they would be happy here. It would certainly not be easy for them as we are a very close-knit community and they would find it difficult to be accepted,' said Mr A. F. Tyler, of Neither Stowey. As for Dulverton, beloved Dulverton where I was born and spent my first formative years, the Rural Councillors believe it would be a 'reversal of help' to offer any Ugandan Asian a home in the Dulverton area.

'If we managed to squeeze them in, there would be nothing for them to do. They want somewhere where they can get down to business,' said the chairman.

Never mind that Dulverton is yearning for someone to revitalise its commercial life and get down to business. Think what effect a little Asian know-how would have on the Women's Institute jumble sales.

When I was a boy, Dulverton was a noisy, thriving community – children were constantly being run over, dog fights were breaking out, there were floods and rowdy Christmas pantomimes in the town hall where local figures were burlesqued without regard to the slander laws. Nowadays, like so many villages, it is populated chiefly by the very old and a sad, mercenary pomposity seems to have descended on it.

Worst of all in the present anti-government frenzy has been the behaviour of Crowcombe Parish Council. Crowcombe is a lovely village at the foot of the Quantocks which recently featured in a BBC documentary about cricket, starring Major T. F. Trollope-Bellow, the squire. It has a splendid mansion, now derelict and allowed to fall into disrepair, and a church with some pew-ends as good as any in Somerset. Sadly enough, on any question it is asked to decide, Crowcombe Parish Council invariably comes down on the side of modernism, ugliness and money. Last week they received a letter from the County Planning Officer which suggested they plant a single broadleaved hardwood tree in the village to replace those lost by the Dutch Elm disease.

Next year has been designated Tree Planting Year and the Department of the Environment is offering fifty per cent grants for the planting of decorative trees. However, Major Trollope-Bellow and other councillors decided that there was no need for this, as their village had plenty of trees already.

I myself have recently lost four beautiful trees – two elms, a beech and a birch. Obviously, without careful planting every year there would be no mature trees left on the property in a hundred years' time. Why is it thought insane nowadays to look so far ahead? If our ancestors had been as selfish and as feckless there would be nothing for us to enjoy now and England would be without what is perhaps her greatest single natural asset.

A splendid body called the Somerset Association of Youth Clubs have been beavering away at this problem for some time, planting 3,000 trees in the county last year. Its organiser, Mrs Henry Hobhouse of Castle Cary, tells me she met furious opposition from tree-haters and modernists but the youths of Somerset have not only planted the trees but kept them weeded and staked as well. Trees, like Ugandan Asians, are being kept out of the countryside simply through suspicion of the Government. All our villages are crying out for a few sharp, brown faces, but the old, the timid and the greedy are in control and there is no help in them.

It would be a wonderful thing if every man, woman and child in England could plant one tree in national Tree Planting Year, justifying to some degree what has been rather a dull generation of Englishmen to date. But at least there will be a few trees left in Somerset, thanks to the Somerset Association of Youth Clubs, long after the last train service has been axed in a desperate last effort to make money.

What an opportunity now opens to plant splendid avenues of oak, elm, beech and chestnut along the old railway tracks.

'Ere Ned, look at them yokels!

Combe Florey, Somerset.

The arrival of a film unit in the Somerset countryside is traditionally the signal for everyone to put on his leather apron and stand by his garden gate, sucking cider through a straw. For a few weeks now, some Independent Artists, as they are apparently called, have been galloping up and down the Quantock Hills shouting 'Tally ho!' at each other and pretending to be country yokels, much to the amazement of the real country yokels, who feel strangely left out of it. The film they are making is an adaptation of a novel by David Rook called *The Ballad of Bellstone Fox*. As its name suggests, it is about a fox, but the film company apparently had the same difficulty with foxes as they had with genuine Somerset yokels.

Whatever qualities the English fox may have, it is quite useless at acting the part of a fox on film, just as yokels can't be trusted to act the part of yokels. All the pubs for miles around are cackling over a story of how the Rank Organisation has been obliged to purchase a consignment of Shelties – miniature Shetland sheepdogs – clip their coats and die them red to play the part of foxes. One of them was very nearly caught by the hounds last week, which would have been a sad episode in a film about a fox which outwits its pursuers and causes the death of the huntsman.

The West Somerset Vale Foxhounds are lending their talents to this enterprise with their Master, Mr Douglas Ayre, and kennel huntsman, Mr Gilbert Down. About a dozen mounted extras have been recruited locally, most of them followers of the hunt. But it is Mr Eric Porter, of Forsyte Saga fame, who steals the show as the film huntsman, with Mr

146

Dennis Waterman as his whipper-in and Rachel Roberts as his lovely wife.

Porter had to learn to ride, virtually from scratch, it appears, and we all hope he is not suffering from blisters on the bottom, a familiar complaint among novice riders and one which is no laughing matter.

The film is causing endless merriment down here, as I may have suggested, but one worries, slightly, whether it will be received in quite the same spirit when shown to a smart London audience. Few people in the country realise the intensity of London's opposition to hunting.

Few Somerset people go anywhere near London, of course, if they can possibly help it. Occasionally, when I have mentioned in London that I come from an area of the country where fox hunting is unquestionably the principal recreation, I have been ordered to explain why I am not prominent in the campaign against cruel sports or leave the room. Although I do not hunt myself, nor do any of my immediate family, it is useless to deny that hunting is a very large part of many people's lives down here, and if I ignore it here for very much longer I will be guilty of wilful deception.

Even the dear old people who come down from Birmingham and Wolverhampton to decorate our countryside with retirement bungalows are sometimes involved, when enraged hounds invade their gardens and frighten their budgerigars or – far, far worse than this – fall on their blameless pussy cats and rend them limb from limb.

Obviously it is not enough to suggest to these bereaved old people that very little happens in their uneventful lives, that they should welcome a little real-life drama, or that the violence they have just witnessed is as nothing to the violence they consume avidly, night after night on television. It is not enough to point out that there is nothing else to do, for many people in the countryside, except chase foxes. There is a strong feeling that the country should be made fit for retired people to live in, and these excesses are no part of most people's retirement plan.

Townspeople are trained to look at the question from the fox's point of view, and it would be futile to deny that the fox has a right to its point of view. Few people in London have probably gone into a chicken house after it has been visited by a fox.

Foxes have an unpleasant habit of killing many more chickens than they can ever possibly hope to eat, usually by biting their heads off. Fox enthusiasts can reasonably point out that chickens are not particularly agreeable birds, and many of them are so stupid that they possibly don't notice whether they are alive or dead. However, non-hunters like myself who have had to clean up after these visits tend to feel noticeably less tender to foxes afterwards.

People refuse to accept as my reason for doing nothing about fox-hunters that I have never particularly cared about chickens. The reason certainly isn't any desire for peace with the neighbours, since country life would be insupportably boring without the occasional fostering of what Harold Wilson used to call creative tensions. The main reason one does nothing about hunting is quite simply that the more one thinks about life, the more difficult it is to condone anything about it.

When townspeople have stopped mugging each other, robbing, ridiculing, suing, and generally trampling each other, I will start wagging my finger at the Master of the West Somerset Vale Foxhounds.

Terrible what zider can do

Combe Florey, Somerset.

The cider harvest is well under way now and already one sees it has been a disastrous year for the cider apple. On top of all our other problems there may well be a world cider shortage in 1973. In France, from where we import a large part of our Somerset cider in the form of unfermented pulp, the price of apples has doubled. Down here, trees which often give sixty to eighty pounds have given four or five.

Somerset may be the traditional place for growing cider apples, but the plain truth is that you can grow them practically anywhere. I often think that the many millions of householders in Britain who have gardens but no interest in gardening should plant them with cider apple trees. They need very little attention, have an agreeable blossom in spring and offer citizens a way round the modern State's greatest single instrument of oppression, its murderous tax on drink.

Fathers of four are particularly vulnerable. Few of us can sit drinking in front of our hungry families with an easy mind, now that food prices are nearly as high as they are on the Continent while drink prices are still two and a half times higher. Yet it is surely fathers of four more than anyone else (except, perhaps, fathers of five and six) who deserve to end the day in a benign haze.

Rough farm cider or 'scrumpy' is not a particularly enjoyable drink, but it is better than nothing. Visitors to Somerset often tell amazing stories of how drunk they have become after two glasses of it, but I think they are mistaken because cider has about the same alcoholic content as beer.

A great deterrent to drunkenness is the effect it has on the stomach – more powerful than syrup of figs. There may be some other ingredient than alcohol which causes intoxication of the brain and paralysis of the legs in visitors to Somerset, but I prefer to think it is the pure Somerset air and unaccustomed exertion which account for these symptoms rather than the cider. Those who seek a benign haze from farm cider must also be prepared for appalling tummy-ache and the same, alas, is true of nearly all home-made wines, whose alcoholic strength is always exaggerated in the telling while their purgative properties are ignored. No doubt that is why the politicians allow us to make them.

Yet I am convinced that it is the murderous price of drink in England which accounts for nearly all the miseries besetting our once-merry land : football hooliganism, colour prejudice, industrial unrest, cynicism about politicians . . . the list is endless. No wonder so many people wish to emigrate.

A few enterprising but misguided young people have been up before the magistrates in Wellington, a few miles from here, accused of growing cannabis plants in their garden. One understands their reason for this behaviour, of course. They seek the tranquillity of mind which alcohol has traditionally afforded in our culture without working themselves to the bone and cluttering the earth's surface with a lot of unnecessary manufactured goods in order to pay for it.

Perhaps cannabis has none of the deleterious effects which the political and directorial classes claim it has. Quite possibly it does not make its adherents blind and mad, like masturbation, or weaken their resistance to Communism, like fluoride in the water. Even so these young people are misguided because the sad fact remains that cannabis grown in Somerset has practically no active ingredient at all.

An average London garden could support six cider apple trees. Once they are planted, nothing need be done to them except prune them every three years. You don't even need to pick the apples, as it doesn't matter if they get bruised in falling. The best cider apples are called Kingston Blacks from the village of Kingston St Mary, where my children go to school, six miles from here. In a good year you might get eighty

pounds of apples from a single tree, enough to make sixty-four pints of cider with a good press. From six trees you could have a pint of cider every day of the year and need never worry about your bowel function again.

Even in National Tree Planting Year, the thought of so much cider may deter a few readers so I shall not reveal the secrets of making it this week. The same amount of cider would make nearly twenty bottles of applejack brandy, but you are sent straight to prison for making that and can be heavily fined even if you possess various household articles which might be assembled to make a still.

Our rulers and would-be rulers claim once again that this is to save us from going blind, or mad, or dying, but those who know tell me that on this occasion they are twisting the facts. It is only wood alcohol which produces deadly poisons, they say, and the worst risk you run in distilling applejack from the 'cheese' left over after apples have been pressed is that a slight variation of temperature will cause a flood of fusel oil into the distillate which, although not toxic, has a most unpleasant taste. Cider itself can be distilled without even this risk.

But it will never be permitted since, if English people could find contentment so easily there would be no incentive to increase their productivity and there would be little for our politicians to preside over for the vital task of boosting their self-importance. Even in France the government is slowly withdrawing the right of peasant farmers to distil their own *eau de vie*.

One method is still legal in England (so long as you don't try to sell the products of it) and that is to freeze your cider, skimming off the ice which forms on top until the total quantity is reduced by about seven eights. As alcohol freezes at a lower temperature than water you are left with a concentration of sorts.

Unfortunately, the sugar and other impurities are similarly concentrated, so the remaining substance may have quite a high alcohol content but will taste of treacle and mud. On the other hand, I don't suppose life is much better in Canada.

Don't be beastly to the squirrel

Combe Florey, Somerset.

The storms of last Sunday week might easily explain why some people still believe in God. A huge elm tree, nine feet thick and almost as old as the house, was the first to go, revealing what one would never have guessed, that it was completely hollow. It took the electricity line with it. Next, a beech brought down the telephone lines.

As we sat in the dark listening to the trees growling and crashing around us, we would have needed to be very hard-hearted not to spare a thought for the poor squirrels inside them. At a time like this, one would have imagined, even the most virulent squirrel-haters might give the poor creatures a rest.

Instead, they seem to have decided that this was the moment for putting the boot in, Last year, I commented on the intemperate language of an English nobleman called Lord Bradford who was using the correspondence columns of *The Times* to attack his own squirrels at Weston Park, Shropshire, in what I thought were most violent and unpleasant terms. Last week he returned to the attack again with another letter to *The Times*.

This time he demanded 'the total outlawing of that immensely destructive pest, the grey squirrel, as otherwise the next generation of hardwood trees and many of the more beautiful conifers will never reach middle age, let alone maturity . . .'

If Lord Bradford is serious when he says that his hardwood trees wrinkle and curl up like lettuces every time they are bitten by a squirrel one can only conclude that he has the most extraordinarily weedy hardwood trees. I have a number of young hardwoods which are the pride and joy of my days.

The squirrels down here eat almost everything – eggs, young birds and even mice, I have been told, although this seems rather beastly – but if any has taken the occasional nibble at my young trees it certainly doesn't show and the trees are going from strength to strength. In another two or three hundred years the park will be as pretty as it was before the storms of last Sunday week.

All this talk of young hardwood trees stripped of their bark and standing naked as film actresses to the wind and the rain is not the voice of reason or science but of fantasy and wild hysteria. Grey squirrels are the most delightful animals if you can overcome the initial panic prompted by terror and mistrust.

Last week another nobleman joined the ranks of squirrel-bashers, Lord Jersey, who wrote from the island of Jersey – where there are no squirrels – with the preposterous suggestion that these dear little animals are responsible for Dutch elm disease. He claims that squirrels keep down the tit population which might otherwise be eating the Dutch elm beetles, and describes in lurid detail the various squirrel-baiting experiments he made as a young man at Osterley Park. However, he adduces no evidence that tits eat these particular beetles, or even that squirrels don't eat them, so I hope that fair-minded people will treat his intervention cautiously.

Dutch elm disease is no joking matter and I am sorry to see people using the horror it arouses to further their personal campaign against grey squirrels. In the same way, silly back-bench MPs often twist any criticism of school milk into a desire to rebuild Belsen and make the working classes starve.

Peter Walker left the Department of the Environment without taking any steps to tackle Dutch elm disease, which is surely the greatest menace to the face of England since the invention of retirement bungalows.

Despite the lavish praise he received from nearly every quarter on his retirement, I must also record that he left the Department without making any decision after the public inquiry on the Quantocks golf course proposals. Now we must address ourselves to Mr Rippon, an unknown quantity in many respects.

Although a native of Surbiton, he was educated at King's College, Taunton, and might, if he was a sensitive lad at the time, have absorbed something of the wild and incredible beauty of the Quantock Hills. To allow the building of a golf course there would be little better than treason, for which men have been hanged fairly recently.

But there is something about Mr Rippon's Mayor-of-Surbiton walk which makes me doubt whether he was ever a very sensitive lad. He might even have been a secret golfer, and the Government's new attitude to squirrels is revealed by last week's edict that in future they may be attacked with rat poison. The future for this once-great country of ours may seem bleak, indeed.

Flooded with kindly thoughts

Combe Florey, Somerset.

Another fortnight of terrible storms. There were rumours at one time that the whole of Midsomer Norton, a large colliery village in the Mendips, had disappeared without trace under the mud like Pompeii under the molten lava of Vesuvius. Bearing in mind the dim view people take nowadays of sightseers at scenes of disaster I did not attempt to copy Pliny the Elder and record the event for posterity. But if the worst has indeed happened, I should strongly advise against any attempts to dig Midsomer Norton up again. Few people know the village well as it is not on any main road, but I went to school a few miles away and until fairly recently I had a pair of maiden great-aunts living there. Now they have been gathered to their Heavenly rest I can honestly assure the world that there was never anything of very great interest to see in Midsomer Norton. Many people may have similar doubts about Pompeii, but about Midsomer Norton they can be sure.

Floods are a regular feature of life in the West Country. Many cottagers round here have had the disagreeable experience of coming downstairs in the morning to find themselves knee-deep in water. Living on the top of a hill, we are protected from the worst consequences and have only choked gutters and fallen trees to contend with, but at the bottom of the hill there is a small lake which forms part of the property. One day this lake is going to burst its banks and flood the whole village, and a quaint local superstition maintains that the owner of the lake is legally responsible for any damage caused. Since one cannot simply remove the lake without a small atom bomb there seems nothing that either side can do except save up our money until the disaster occurs and then pay it all to lawyers for the benefit of learned arguments about the rights and wrongs of the matter.

One solution might be to launch a public subscription. It is very seldom that anybody takes an interest in our West Country disasters, but when people do the results are quite impressive. After the Lynmouth flood disaster of 1952 public response was extremely generous, and word got round among the farmers that anyone who had lost a chicken in the flood would be able to buy himself a cow from the compensation. Probably this was quite wrong, but I fear many chickens came to an untimely end in various bathrooms and kitchens sinks while the rumour ran its course.

My own memory of the Lynmouth flood is much happier. Hastening to the scene of the disaster with various sisters and cousins – the oldest could not have been more than fourteen – we were met by a huge black man who gave us each a bunch of bananas. It turned out that the President of Ghana or someone like that had very kindly sent a consignment of bananas to relieve the distress of flood victims. My fellow ghouls and I were filmed eating them for the benefit of the Ghanaians, all of us grinning like lunatics. I believe the Prime Minister of Australia also sent a boat-load of kangaroo skins, although I never got one of them.